'Hand has written a book on the deeply difficult problem of moral education that is a marvel of clarity and cogency. He never succumbs to the evasiveness or the dogmatism that almost always undermines writing on this topic. When he takes a stand, you will always understand the reasons why he does so, even if you disagree with him. No recent book on the topic can compare with this one.'

Eamonn Callan, Pigott Family Professor of Education, Stanford University, USA

'This groundbreaking book should become essential reading for anyone interested in moral education in modern multicultural societies. It is written in a straightforward, direct style, and is packed with careful arguments. Whether or not you agree with Hand's arguments, you'll come away with a much better understanding of what is at stake. Highly recommended.'

Harry Brighouse, Professor of Philosophy, University of Wisconsin-Madison, USA

A THEORY OF MORAL EDUCATION

Children must be taught morality. They must be taught to recognise the authority of moral standards and to understand what makes them authoritative. But there's a problem: the content and justification of morality are matters of reasonable disagreement among reasonable people. This makes it hard to see how educators can secure children's commitment to moral standards without indoctrinating them.

In *A Theory of Moral Education*, Michael Hand tackles this problem head on. He sets out to show that moral education can and should be fully rational. It is true that many moral standards and justificatory theories are controversial, and educators have an obligation to teach these *nondirectively*, with the aim of enabling children to form their own considered views. But reasonable moral disagreement does not go all the way down: some basic moral standards are robustly justified, and these should be taught *directively*, with the aim of bringing children to recognise and understand their authority.

This is an original and important contribution to the philosophy of moral education, which lays a new theoretical foundation for the urgent practical task of teaching right from wrong.

Michael Hand is Professor of Philosophy of Education at the University of Birmingham, UK.

A THEORY OF MORAL EDUCATION

Michael Hand

Routledge
Taylor & Francis Group

LONDON AND NEW YORK

First published 2018
by Routledge
2 Park Square, Milton Park, Abingdon, Oxon OX14 4RN

and by Routledge
711 Third Avenue, New York, NY 10017

Routledge is an imprint of the Taylor & Francis Group, an informa business

© 2018 Michael Hand

The right of Michael Hand to be identified as author of this work has been
asserted by him in accordance with sections 77 and 78 of the Copyright, Designs
and Patents Act 1988.

British Library Cataloguing in Publication Data
A catalogue record for this book is available from the British Library

Library of Congress Cataloging in Publication Data
A catalog record for this book has been requested

ISBN: 978-1-138-89853-0 (hbk)
ISBN: 978-1-138-89854-7 (pbk)
ISBN: 978-1-315-70850-8 (ebk)

Typeset in Bembo
by Taylor & Francis Books

For Al, Nick and Ed

CONTENTS

PREFACE

The theory I present in this book has had a long gestation period. The problem it purports to solve, or at least some inchoate version of the problem, has troubled me since the beginning of my academic career. In my first few published articles I explored the threat of indoctrination in religious education and upbringing (Hand, 2002, 2003, 2004a, 2004b). I argued, and still hold, that to indoctrinate someone is to bring it about that she holds beliefs non-rationally, on some other basis than relevant evidence and argument, and that indoctrination should be avoided by educators. That puts a severe constraint on what is permissible in the domain of religious education and upbringing. But it also has implications for *moral* education and upbringing, in particular for attempts to impart beliefs about the authority of moral standards.

I first articulated the problem in roughly the form it takes here in a keynote presentation at the 2010 Annual Conference of the Philosophy of Education Society of Great Britain. I did not, at that point, attempt to solve it. The week after that conference I departed for a five-month stint as a visiting scholar at Stanford University, confident that I would return to the UK with a solution to the problem and a draft of this book. Despite illuminating conversations with Eamonn Callan, Rob Reich, Susan Verducci and Michael Katz, and long days in the Green Library chasing promising philosophical leads, I came home, much chastened, with neither.

The project went on hold for a while until, in 2012, I moved from the London Institute of Education to the University of Birmingham and began a three-year affiliation with the Jubilee Centre for Character and Virtues. There, in the stimulating philosophical company of Randall Curren, Ben Kotzee, Kristján Kristjánsson and David Carr, I resumed work on the problem and the argument of this book began to take shape. I first presented the theory, in prototypical form, in my inaugural lecture at Birmingham in January 2014 (Hand, 2014).

Still, writing did not begin in earnest until my next period of study leave, in 2016. Four months holed up in an empty library on Birmingham's ghost-town Selly Oak campus brought me within sight of the finishing line – though it took me almost another year to cross it. So the text that follows has been some 15 years in the making. Fortunately for the project, and unfortunately for moral educators and their students, the problem of how to teach morality rationally has become no less pressing in the interim.

In addition to the people already mentioned, others who have discussed with me and helped me to refine the ideas in this book are David Aldridge, Philip Hand, Anders Schinkel, Harvey Siegel, Judith Suissa, John Tillson, John Vorhaus, John White and Patricia White. Most of them, I should add, disagree with me quite vehemently.

Three people deserve special thanks. David Copp has been a huge influence on my thinking and a willing correspondent. A lengthy email exchange and a meeting in London in 2011 were epiphanic. I take some small credit for persuading David to turn his own attention to moral education, the first fruit of which has recently appeared in print (Copp, 2016). Randall Curren has encouraged me in this project from the outset and been a constant source of support, inspiration, advice and friendship. And Laura D'Olimpio, my book buddy, has kept me company over the last 14 months of intensive writing, commenting on my draft chapters, talking me through sticking points and lifting my spirits when they flagged. Annoyingly, she has pipped me to the post: her own book on moral education (D'Olimpio, 2017) is published just a few weeks before this one.

Thanks, finally, to my four hard-to-impress housemates: to my wife, Carol, for her endless impatience with such scholarly indulgences as crises of confidence and writer's block; and to my sons, Al, Nick and Ed, for caring not a hoot about what Dad does when they're at school. It has helped more than they know to be reminded daily that this is, after all, just a book.

MJH
June 2017

1

REASONABLE DISAGREEMENT ABOUT MORALITY

People disagree about morality. They disagree about what morality prohibits, permits and requires. And they disagree about *why* morality prohibits, permits and requires these things. Moreover, at least some of the disagreement on these matters is reasonable. It is not readily attributable to woolly thinking or ignorance or inattention to relevant considerations. Sensible and sincere people armed with similar life experience and acquainted with roughly the same facts come to notably different conclusions about the content and justification of morality.

I shall argue in this chapter that reasonable disagreement about morality presents a significant challenge to the enterprise of moral education. And in the rest of the book I shall set out a theory of moral education that, I hope, meets this challenge. I think the theory meets some other challenges faced by moral educators too; but it is the problem of reasonable disagreement that provides the impetus for my inquiry and that I consider to be most urgently in need of a solution.

The problem, baldly stated, is this. It is hard to see how we can bring it about that children subscribe to moral standards, and believe them to be justified, except by giving them some form of moral education. But it is also hard to see how moral educators can legitimately cultivate such subscription and belief in the face of reasonable disagreement about the content and justification of morality. It looks as though any attempt to persuade children of the authority of a selected moral code, when there are perfectly respectable alternatives available, is bound to be indoctrinatory.

The standard responses to this problem are as familiar as they are inadequate. We might deny that morality needs to be taught, putting our faith in the natural goodness of children or their propensity to identify and subscribe to moral standards of their own accord. Or we might bite the indoctrination bullet and resolve to inculcate a selected moral code and associated justification, relying on manipulation and misrepresentation to prevent serious consideration of the alternatives. Or we might decline to educate *in* morality and simply educate *about* it, inviting children to reflect critically on a range of moral codes and associated justifications and decide for themselves which, if any, merits their compliance.

Perhaps the severity of the problem and the inadequacy of the standard responses will be immediately granted. In case they are not, however, let me say a little more about each.

Reasonable moral disagreement

Reasonable disagreement is possible where the evidence and argument bearing on a matter is subject to more than one plausible interpretation. If people disagree on a matter because their plausible interpretations of the relevant evidence and argument conflict, their disagreement is a reasonable one. It does not follow, of course, that all disagreements about matters on which reasonable disagreement is possible are in fact reasonable: there are plenty of people who hold rationally untenable views on rationally contentious issues. Still, the plethora of questions to which we do not know the answer, and to which more than one possible answer has something to be said for it, makes reasonable disagreement a pervasive feature of our lives.

We may distinguish two kinds of reasonable disagreement in the sphere of morality. The first kind has to do with the *application* of moral standards to particular cases. People who subscribe to the same moral code with the same justification may not agree on what is morally required of them in a given situation. One reason for this is that moral norms sometimes make conflicting demands: it seems to be true of more or less any moral code that its adherents will occasionally find themselves in situations where compliance with one moral norm necessitates non-compliance with another. Consider, for example, a moral code that prohibits both lying and causing distress to others. Adherents of the code agree that lying and causing distress should be avoided wherever possible; they agree, too, that telling a white lie is normally preferable to hurting someone's feelings, and that causing minor distress is normally preferable to concealing important information. Because of this agreement, they will usually reach the same verdict on what is morally required in situations to which one or both of the prohibitions apply. But some situations in which telling the truth involves causing distress are plainly not covered by the agreed guidelines: namely, situations in which the truth matters and the distress caused is likely to be great. Here adherents of the code confront a *moral dilemma*. They see that it matters, morally speaking, which course of action they choose; but they lack an agreed procedure for weighing the relevant moral considerations against each other. Moral dilemmas are therefore one source of reasonable disagreement about the application of moral standards.

Another reason for moral disagreement of this first kind is that it is sometimes difficult to decide whether a given action is of a morally prohibited or required type. Suppose an act of appropriation meets some but not all of the criteria we use to identify instances of theft. There are currently, on my bookshelf, three or four volumes I am fairly sure I acquired originally from people who lent them to me in the expectation that they would be returned. At the time of borrowing them, I no doubt intended to return them, though in a fairly weak sense of 'intended'. It would perhaps be more accurate to say that I did not intend not to return them. Nevertheless, they were not returned, and I now have neither a clear recollection of who lent me the books nor much inclination to investigate the matter with a view to restoring them to their rightful owners. Am I guilty of theft? The question is one on which there is room for reasonable disagreement among people who agree that stealing is morally wrong (and, indeed, on which there is room for a moral agent to be divided within himself: I do occasionally feel guilty about the volumes on my shelf, and my guilt is only partly assuaged by the thought that I have lost more books by this route than I have gained). In the main, of course, it is perfectly obvious when an act of appropriation is a case of stealing, and more generally when a given action is of a morally prohibited or required type; but it is not always perfectly obvious, and sometimes it is very unclear.

Reasonable disagreement about the application of moral standards – the kind of disagreement that arises from moral dilemmas and borderline cases of morally regulated actions – is an important feature of moral life and a proper focus of attention for moral educators. But it is not this kind of disagreement that threatens the enterprise of moral education: it presents no impediment to teaching children an authoritative moral code. The threat to moral education is posed by reasonable moral disagreement of the second kind: disagreement about the *content* and *justification* of morality. Sometimes people reasonably disagree not about the application of moral standards they share, but about which moral standards are authoritative and why.

Are citizens of democratic states morally required to vote in general elections? Is it morally wrong to eat meat? Are parents morally permitted to smack their children? People disagree about the answers to these questions. Some recognise a moral requirement to vote, or a moral prohibition on eating meat or smacking children; others recognise no such requirement or prohibition. Those in the latter camp may, of course, vote because they care about politics, follow a vegetarian diet for health reasons, or refrain from smacking because they consider it an ineffective form of discipline; but here they are acting on the basis of non-moral practical judgments, not complying with moral standards. When people disagree about the moral regulation of voting, meat-eating and smacking, they are disagreeing about the content of morality; and their disagreement is quite reasonable. It is plausible to argue that membership and enjoyment of the benefits of a democratically governed society confer a moral obligation to participate in the democratic process. But it is also plausible to argue that political freedom includes the moral right not to participate in the democratic process if one prefers not to. It is even plausible to suggest that those who cannot make an informed judgment in the polling booth – because they have not troubled to find out about the candidates or think through the implications of their policies – have a moral obligation *not* to vote. In the same way, there are sensible things to be said both for and against the claims that meat-eating and smacking are morally wrong.

To be sure, not all moral standards are as controversial as the ones that regulate voting, meat-eating and smacking. There is much less disagreement, for example, about the authority of moral prohibitions on lying, cheating and stealing. Perhaps we might identify a core of basic moral standards endorsed by more or less all reasonable people. If there is such a consensus, it is a fact of no little importance; but we are not yet out of the woods. For agreement on the content of a moral code does not entail agreement on its justification. And, in fact, justificatory arguments for even the most universally recognised moral standards are fiercely contested.

Take the widely accepted moral prohibition on lying. Most of us think we always have a pro tanto moral reason not to lie, even if that reason is sometimes defeated by countervailing considerations of greater weight. But it is far from clear that we accept the same justification for our shared moral standard. No doubt it is rare for many of us to consider the question of *why* lying is wrong; but when we do consider it, we find ourselves confronted with a plethora of possible answers. One suggestion is that we should not lie because general compliance with a prohibition on lying is conducive to the greatest happiness for the greatest number. Another is that, when we tell someone a lie, we treat her not as an end-in-herself, but as a means to our ends: we manipulate her by our deception and thus fail to respect her dignity as a person. A third is that possessing and exercising the virtue of honesty is a necessary condition of our own flourishing. A fourth is that lying is wrong because it subverts the proper function of speech, which is to communicate to others what is in our minds. And a fifth is that, in view of our limited capacity to make sense of the human condition, we do better to rely on the guidance of an omniscient divine being in matters of morality, and it so happens that such a being has reliably informed us that we ought not to lie. Alongside this diverse range of justificatory strategies sits another possibility: the thought that a rational justification for our shared moral standard is unavailable. It is a fact about most of us that we are disposed to refrain from lying, to feel guilty when we do lie, and to disapprove of lies told by others. We can speculate about the biological and environmental *causes* of this disposition, but it is a mistake to suppose that we shall be able to find a *justification* for it. It is just what human beings are like.

I do not suggest that all these responses to the question of why lying is wrong are equally credible. But they are all familiar proposals in moral theory; some of them are at least plausible; and none can fairly be said to settle the matter. Even if there is consensus among reasonable people on some basic moral standards, there seems to be little consensus on what, if anything, grounds those standards. Agreement reached at the level of content falls apart at the level of justification.

That reasonable disagreement of this second kind – disagreement about the content and justification of morality – is a salient feature of contemporary societies, and that it presents those societies with significant challenges, is a key premise of much recent political philosophy. John Rawls famously formulates the fundamental question of political justice like this: 'how is it possible for there to exist over time a just and stable society of free and equal citizens who remain profoundly divided by reasonable religious, philosophical and moral doctrines?' (Rawls, 2005, p.4).

And he contends that the profound divides between reasonable citizens on matters of religion and morality are unlikely to be closed any time soon:

> The political culture of a democratic society is always marked by a diversity of opposing and irreconcilable religious, philosophical and moral doctrines. Some of these are perfectly reasonable, and this diversity among reasonable doctrines political liberalism sees as the inevitable long-run result of the powers of human reason at work within the background of enduring free institutions.
>
> *(ibid., pp.3–4)*

Human beings, exercising their powers of reason in the absence of coercion, will come to different conclusions on matters of morality because the relevant evidence and argument is subject to more than one plausible interpretation. The Rawlsian worry is that this casts doubt on the possibility of a just and stable society of free and equal citizens; my interest here is in the doubt it casts on the possibility of a defensible form of moral education.

The threat to moral education

The problem for moral education posed by reasonable disagreement about morality consists in the difficulty of reconciling the following three claims:

1. Moral education aims to bring it about that children subscribe to moral standards and believe them to be justified.
2. There is reasonable disagreement about the content and justification of morality.
3. Teaching propositions as true, or standards as justified, when there is reasonable disagreement about them, is indoctrinatory.

It seems to follow from the conjunction of these three claims that moral educators have no defensible means of realising their ends. They are tasked with ensuring that children recognise the authority of a moral code, but they cannot fulfil that task without resorting to impermissible methods of teaching. I have indicated above why I think we should be sympathetic to claim (2). What about claims (1) and (3)?

The aim of bringing about subscription to moral standards and belief in their justification is not a *necessary* one for moral educators. Teaching about moral codes, in the sense of explaining what they require and how they differ, without any thought of persuading children that one or other of them is authoritative, is a perfectly intelligible undertaking, and one for which 'moral education' is not an inappropriate label. But moral education understood merely as the anthropological study of moral codes would hardly answer to the pressing social need most of us take to be the raison d'être of the enterprise. Moral education matters because each new generation must be taught the difference between right and wrong; children must come to understand and be disposed to comply with the requirements of morality. The crucial educational task is the formation of responsible moral agents, and this *does* involve the cultivation of subscription to moral standards and belief in their justification.

Note that I am not concerned at this point with the division of educational labour between home and school. Suppose it were to be proposed that the formation of responsible moral agents should take place in the home and the anthropological study of moral codes in the school. Well, then the conundrum I have identified is one faced by parents rather than teachers. I take it that parents, no less than teachers, have an obligation not to indoctrinate, so relieving schools of responsibility for the hard part of moral education is no solution to the problem. (In fact I think this hypothetical division of moral educational labour would be highly impractical: parents and teachers are jointly responsible for ensuring that children recognise the authority of a moral code, so face the conundrum together.)

The claim that it is indoctrinatory to teach propositions as true, or standards as justified, when there is reasonable disagreement about them is a familiar one in the literature on indoctrination. To indoctrinate someone is to impart beliefs to her in such a way that she comes to hold them non-rationally, on some other basis than the force of relevant evidence and argument. Propositions or standards about which there is reasonable disagreement are those for which the relevant evidence and argument is subject to more than one plausible interpretation. If a teacher wishes to persuade a learner that such propositions are true, or such standards justified, she cannot do so by rational demonstration, by producing compelling evidence or decisive arguments. She must instead resort to non-rational means of persuasion, to some form of manipulation or psychological pressure, to bring about the desired beliefs. But beliefs into which a learner has been cajoled, bullied or seduced are beliefs she has come to hold on a basis other than the force of relevant evidence and argument. They are, that is to say, beliefs into which she has been indoctrinated.

It is sometimes suggested that teaching cannot be indoctrinatory unless there is an *intention*, on the part of the teacher, to bring it about that learners hold beliefs non-rationally. If this were true, moral educators could avoid the charge of indoctrination merely by eschewing this intention. They could overcome the threat to moral education by persuading themselves that they have, and can give to learners, conclusive reasons for believing that certain moral standards are justified, even if conclusive reasons are in fact unavailable. As I am using the term 'indoctrinatory' here, there need not, and often will not, be any intention on the part of the teacher that learners should come to hold beliefs non-rationally. What makes teaching indoctrinatory is that learners *do* come to hold beliefs in this way, whatever the teacher's intention. The problem for moral education is that beliefs about which there is reasonable disagreement can only be reliably imparted to others in ways that result in their being non-rationally held.

Indoctrination is considered a significant harm because of the difficulty of shifting beliefs one has come to hold non-rationally. Insofar as beliefs are held on the basis of evidence and argument, they are open to revision and correction. One is prepared to modify or relinquish them in the light of fresh evidence, or fresh appraisals of old evidence. Insofar as beliefs are held non-rationally, on the other hand, they are highly resistant to reassessment. Because they are not founded on evidence and argument, the discovery of counter-evidence and counter-argument has little or no effect on them. The damage done to the child's mind by indoctrinatory teaching is well-described by John Wilson:

> For here we have taken over, or put to sleep, a central part of the child's personality – his ability to think rationally in a certain area. To put it dramatically: there is always hope so long as the mind remains free, however much our behaviour may be forced or our feelings conditioned. But if we occupy the inner citadel of thought and language, then it is difficult to see how a person can develop or regain rationality except by a very lengthy and arduous course of treatment.
>
> *(Wilson et al., 1967, pp.174–175)*

Teachers, parents and others involved in the education of children ought to be both implacably opposed to indoctrination and acutely aware of how easy it is to slip, consciously or unconsciously, from rational to non-rational means of persuasion in the transmission of beliefs. But anyone so opposed and aware cannot fail to be troubled by the aim of bringing it about, in the face of reasonable disagreement about morality, that children subscribe to moral standards and believe them to be justified.

Doing without moral education

One standard response to this problem is the proposal that we simply abandon the enterprise of moral education. The thought here is that we can sidestep the difficulty of teaching morality by recognising that morality is usually caught rather than taught, or perhaps that it is innate rather than acquired. If teaching morality is unnecessary, we need not look too hard for a defensible way of doing it.

Take, first, the suggestion that morality is caught rather than taught. This looks quite plausible if it is taken to mean that most significant moral learning takes place informally, in the context of children's real-life encounters with situations to which moral standards apply, rather than formally, in the context of methodical instruction or theoretical exposition in the classroom. Learning morality is not much like learning maths or music, and this is reflected in the fact that, unlike maths and music, it rarely features as a discrete subject on school curricula. But this way of interpreting the distinction between 'caught' and 'taught' lends no support at all to the idea that teaching morality is unnecessary: it shows, at most, that the kind of teaching involved in moral education differs from the kind of teaching involved in traditional curriculum subjects.

To support the conclusion that moral education is redundant, the claim that morality is caught rather than taught must be taken to mean that children's moral learning requires no deliberate facilitation by adults. Because children can be relied upon to pick up morality for themselves, the adults responsible for their education need play no part in bringing it about that they recognise the authority of a moral code. On this view, learning morality is akin to learning gender stereotypes: just as children internalise messages about the different kinds of behaviour expected of boys and girls without any deliberate reinforcement of those messages by their parents and teachers, so they internalise without pedagogical assistance messages about the requirements and authority of morality.

But on this interpretation the claim looks much less plausible. The phenomenon of children internalising gender stereotypes in the absence of efforts by parents and teachers to reinforce them, and even in the teeth of active efforts to undermine them, is a familiar one; the phenomenon of children learning morality without the assistance of parents and teachers is rather less familiar. Moral instruction and guidance is so integral to our understanding of parenting and teaching that it is hard to imagine what these activities would look like without it. Chastising children for hurting each other, for telling lies, for cheating in tests or stealing from shops, with a view to cultivating in them dispositions not to do these things, to feel guilty for doing them, and to disapprove when they are done by others, is a more or less universal feature of upbringing. Morality is always, in practice, taught as well as caught; and while it does not follow from this that morality *must* be taught, nor do we have any good reason to think that teaching is dispensable. Conscientious compliance with moral standards is, after all, a very different sort of learning outcome from unthinking conformity with gender stereotypes. The most striking difference, perhaps, is that morality conflicts much more sharply and frequently than gender stereotypes with children's immediate desires and preferences. Adhering to moral norms requires children to resist powerful temptations to lash out at those who annoy them, or take what does not belong to them, and it seems doubtful that they would learn to resist these temptations without the incentives supplied by moral chastisement and training. Adhering to gender norms, by contrast, is typically much less motivationally demanding, much less incongruent with children's immediate desires and wants (which is not, of course, to deny that it may be harmful to them, or that their desires themselves may be inauthentically gendered). This asymmetry should make us wary of supposing that moral learning can be left to take care of itself.

What about the more radical suggestion that morality is innate rather than acquired? Such appeal as this view has rests on the thought that human beings are social animals: we are constituted by nature to live in social groups, to derive pleasure from friendship and social interaction, to empathise and sympathise with others, and to solve problems by cooperation. I think we *are* so constituted, and evolutionary psychologists have plausible stories to tell about why we should have evolved in this way. But it is a serious mistake to confuse natural sympathy and prosocial motivation with morality. To have a moral code is to subscribe, in a particular way, to standards of conduct that prohibit and require actions of certain kinds. Insofar as we help those in need simply because we are distressed by their plight, or refrain from violence just because we find it unpleasant, our motivation is not properly described as moral. We are morally motivated to the extent that we are moved to help those in need and refrain from violence by our subscription to a moral code that requires these things. And while it may be true that human beings could not be persuaded to subscribe to moral codes in the first place if they were not naturally sympathetic to one another, this fact, if it is a fact, does nothing to erode the distinction between morality and sympathy.

Once it is recognised that morality involves action regulated by standards to which one subscribes, and not merely action motivated by sympathy or prosocial sentiment, the appeal of the suggestion that morality is innate quickly evaporates. It must, of course, be true that we are biologically equipped with a *capacity* for morality, just as we must be equipped with a capacity for language; but we are no more born subscribing to a moral code than we are born fluent in a mother tongue. Morality and language are rule-governed social practices into which infant human beings must be initiated.

Morality is acquired rather than innate and must be taught as well as caught; so giving up on moral education is no solution to the problem of reasonable disagreement about morality.

Biting the indoctrination bullet

A second standard response to the problem is to accept that indoctrination is unavoidable in the moral sphere. Confronted with both reasonable disagreement about the content and justification of morality and an obligation to bring it about that children subscribe to moral standards and believe them to be justified, we have no choice but to resort to non-rational means of persuasion. If we could impart beliefs about what morality requires and why by furnishing children with compelling evidence or decisive arguments, we should of course do so; but we cannot do that, and it is preferable to indoctrinate beliefs of this kind than to leave children without them. There are, after all, worse things than being indoctrinated.

A familiar analogue of this argument for non-rational moral education is found in debates about confessional religious education. It is widely accepted, by both advocates and opponents of confessional religious education, that religious beliefs are matters of reasonable disagreement and therefore cannot be imparted to others by means of rational demonstration. But advocates maintain that to raise children without a set of religious beliefs and values is to deny them access to an important dimension of human experience and a rich source of meaning and purpose in life. So valuable is this educational end, they say, that it justifies such means of imparting religious beliefs as catechism and evangelism, compulsory participation in prayer, worship and liturgy, rewards for orthodoxy and punishments for heresy, marginalisation and misrepresentation of alternative perspectives, and the construction of curricula that presuppose rather than problematise the favoured beliefs.

Indeed, some versions of this case for confessional religious education are not so much analogues of the argument for non-rational moral education as instances of it. Adherence to a religion typically involves both subscription to a set of moral standards and acceptance of a theological justification for them, so to cultivate religious commitment in children is also to realise the central aims of moral education. And it is not uncommon for advocates of confessional religious education to foreground its specifically moral outcomes in their attempts to justify the use of non-rational means of persuasion. The indoctrinatory methods employed by some religious parents, schools and communities should be permitted, it is argued, precisely because they are effective in bringing it about that children subscribe to moral standards and believe them to be justified.

Those willing to endorse non-rational belief transmission in the moral and religious spheres tend to underestimate the harmfulness of indoctrination. Preferring that children come to hold beliefs rationally rather than non-rationally is not like preferring that they come to write neatly rather than messily, or to argue tightly rather than loosely. A non-rationally-held belief is not just a rough-and-ready version of a rationally-held one. Rather, holding beliefs on a topic non-rationally is a serious impediment to thinking clearly about that topic, to engaging critically and open-mindedly with evidence and argument bearing on it, and to moderating or relinquishing beliefs that turn out to be unwarranted. Indoctrinated beliefs are thought-stoppers, and we do children a major disservice by stopping their thinking in areas of such immense personal and interpersonal significance as morality and religion.

Supporters of non-rational moral education also tend to overestimate the stability of indoctrinated beliefs. This may seem a surprising objection, given that some influential analyses of the concept of indoctrination have made unshakeability a necessary feature of indoctrinated beliefs (e.g. White, 1967). But beliefs held non-rationally are not unshakeable; they are not even particularly stable. Children who are indoctrinated with the moral or religious views of their parents or teachers routinely cast off those views when they reach adolescence or adulthood, not because they have examined the epistemic credentials of the views and found them wanting, but because they are rejecting or rebelling against the pedagogical power exercised over them. Beliefs into which one has been cajoled, bullied or seduced remain tied up with the psychological hold of the people doing the cajoling, bullying or seducing; to break free of that hold is to deprive those beliefs of their chief support, which not infrequently results in their abandonment. Indoctrinated beliefs are for this reason notably less stable than beliefs imparted by rational demonstration: insofar as one believes something because the evidence for it is compelling, one is only likely to withdraw one's assent if the evidence is subsequently overturned or superseded. Of course that happens sometimes, but the evidential support for rationally-held beliefs is not nearly as transient or volatile as the psychological support for non-rationally-held ones. So, while indoctrinatory methods can certainly be used to persuade children of the authority of a moral code, the stability of the resulting beliefs leaves much to be desired.

Still, even if indoctrination bullet-biters can be convicted of insouciance about the dangers of their proposal, their basic point remains unanswered. Their claim is not that indoctrination is harmless: it is that, confronted with a choice between indoctrinating beliefs about the content and justification of morality and leaving children without such beliefs, we should opt for the former as the lesser of two evils. It may be true that indoctrinated beliefs do more harm, and are less stable, than is often assumed, but this hardly undermines the claim that indoctrination is a lesser evil than amorality. If these really were the only two options open to us, we should perhaps, in the end, be forced to concede the bullet-biters' point. In the chapters that follow I shall try to show that these are *not* the only options available.

Educating about morality

A third and final standard response to the problem of reasonable disagreement is the suggestion that we educate children *about* morality rather than *in* it. On this view we should make children aware of a broad range of moral codes and justificatory arguments, encourage them to subject those codes and arguments to critical scrutiny, and invite them to subscribe to whichever code they take to enjoy the strongest argumentative support. We should neither assume that children will learn morality unaided, nor presume to impose on them the moral code we happen to favour: our job as educators is to cultivate moral autonomy by enabling children to make their own independent judgments on the content and justification of morality.

This argument for neutral moral education also has a familiar analogue in debates about the teaching of religion, this time in a prominent case for non-confessional religious education. Because religious beliefs are matters of reasonable disagreement and cannot be imparted to others by rational means, we have no business trying to persuade children of their truth. But because religious claims are momentous, in the sense of bearing directly on fundamental questions about the meaning and purpose of life, children have a right to be acquainted with them and equipped with the wherewithal to evaluate them. So parents and teachers have a responsibility to teach religion as impartially as possible, with a view to fostering religious autonomy rather than religious faith.

The case for non-confessional religious education is, I think, compelling: when it comes to religious creeds, we should indeed educate about rather than in. But it is less clear that this is a viable approach to the teaching of moral codes. One worry is that, by delaying children's subscription to moral standards until such time as they are in a position to choose it for themselves, we uncomfortably extend the period of childhood amorality. The fact that infants do not yet subscribe to moral prohibitions on violence, deception and theft is harmless enough, given their incapacity to cause much injury to those around them; but children of school age who do not subscribe to these prohibitions pose rather more of a threat to their communities. For reasons of public safety, it seems, we can ill afford an approach to moral education that permits children to remain amoral until they can autonomously endorse a moral code.

This worry may not be decisive. There are, after all, more kinds of authority than moral authority. Children can be persuaded to comply with prohibitions on violence, deception and theft without being persuaded that these are requirements of morality. School rules that prohibit running in corridors or wearing jewellery in gymnastics lessons are not moral; nor are house rules that require homework before TV or putting dirty socks in the laundry basket. By introducing prohibitions on antisocial behaviour as school rules or house rules in the first instance, we can perhaps secure children's compliance with them while leaving open the question of whether or not they are morally authoritative.

There is, however, another worry about neutral moral education that is less easily assuaged. It seems likely that, once children come to appreciate that there are different moral codes supported by different justificatory arguments, and that disagreement on these matters is reasonable, the option of remaining morally agnostic will be at least as attractive as the option of plumping for one or other of the available moral doctrines. Some, no doubt, will judge one account of the content and justification of morality to be correct, and will be moved to subscribe to the standards it purports to justify (or, perhaps, to convert their non-moral subscription to moral subscription); but others will find themselves unable to choose sensibly between the accounts before them and will simply defer judgment until such time as the reasonable disagreement about morality has been satisfactorily resolved. This, after all, is how things typically go with non-confessional religious education. The objection to non-confessional religious education most frequently advanced by its critics is that it nudges children in the direction of agnosticism. Confronted with a dizzying array of religious creeds and supporting theological arguments and invited to choose between them, the natural and predictable response of many children is to decline the invitation, to withhold religious judgment in the absence of a decisive reason to favour one creed over the others.

Merely educating about morality, then, not only extends the period of childhood amorality to the point at which children are capable of autonomous moral choice, but also predictably results in some children autonomously choosing to be morally agnostic. It is, therefore, a form of moral education inadequate to the task of reliably bringing it about that children subscribe to moral standards and believe them to be justified.

It is important to distinguish the view that moral education *per se* should be neutral between rival moral doctrines from the view that moral education *in schools* should be neutral. It is the former view that we have been discussing here. The latter view, insofar as it is paired with the thought that parents are at liberty to inculcate their preferred moral doctrine in the home, is really just a version of the indoctrinatory model of moral education considered in the previous section. Schools serving morally diverse communities, in which people subscribe to different moral codes for different reasons, can best assist parents in passing on their moral views by, so to speak, staying out of the way. Schools that are either silent on moral matters, or tackle them from a position of strict neutrality, avoid contaminating the indoctrinatory processes underway in homes. At best, by making children aware of alternative moral codes and justificatory arguments, schools offer them the possibility of rejecting the doctrines their parents have chosen for them; for the most part, though, school neutrality serves only to ensure that non-rational parental moral influence is largely unchecked.

The plight of the moral educator

I have argued that the threat to moral education posed by reasonable disagreement about morality is a serious one, and that none of the standard responses to this threat is satisfactory. The problem is not solved by giving up on moral education, by biting the indoctrination bullet or by teaching moral codes neutrally.

I do not suggest that parents and teachers are oblivious to the shortcomings of the standard responses. To the contrary, I think most are aware, some acutely, others dimly, that none of the readily available options is educationally adequate. Few parents or teachers are dogmatically committed to the idea that morality is innate rather than acquired, or caught rather than taught, or to the non-rational inculcation of moral standards, or to the sufficiency of educating about morality. Rather, seeing no other alternative, most shift uneasily back and forth between these options, resting with each just long enough to be reminded of its deficiencies. This is meant not as a criticism of those with responsibility for the moral education of children, but as a description of their plight: neither parents nor teachers have a clear sense of what they are supposed to be doing in this area.

To the extent that this captures the plight of the moral educator, the theory I shall develop in the chapters that follow is *practitioner-aligned*. An educational theory is practitioner-aligned when the question it purports to answer, or the problem it purports to solve, is one recognised by and troubling to practitioners; it is practitioner-unaligned when the question or problem it addresses is one that practitioners either do not recognise or are not troubled by. Practitioner-aligned theories speak directly to the existing concerns of those engaged in a practice; practitioner-unaligned theories speak past such concerns, on the grounds that the things practitioners worry about are not the only things that matter.

There is no presumption in favour of practitioner-aligned educational theories. It would drastically and damagingly restrict the scope of educational scholarship if the research agenda were set wholly by the practical difficulties of parents and teachers. As Robert Dearden remarks,

> it is important for theory not to be entirely governed by pragmatic relevance, first, because that would put the purpose or ends of current practice themselves beyond theoretical criticism; and secondly, because in being so governed by practice, theory could very easily become mere apologetic ideology.
>
> *(Dearden, 1984, p.10)*

But nor, by the same token, is practitioner-alignment something to be frowned upon. At least one of the reasons for having educational theorists around is the prospect of their shedding useful light on the problems faced by educational practitioners. Plainly there is little merit in removing impediments to the pursuit of misconceived educational goals; but where the goals are in order, such assistance as theorists can offer in facilitating their pursuit is surely to be welcomed.

Theorists whose concerns coincide with those of practitioners enjoy an obvious advantage when it comes to influencing practice. Practitioners are naturally more attentive to theories that purport to help them with difficulties they acknowledge than to theories that do not. It is my hope that parents and teachers will be interested in the theory advanced in this book because they are genuinely struggling with the problem it tries to solve. Insofar as they hold that children must be brought to subscribe to moral standards and believe them to be justified, that there is reasonable disagreement about the content and justification of morality, and that teaching propositions as true, or standards as justified, when there is reasonable disagreement about them, is indoctrinatory, they can hardly avoid the conundrum presented by the conjunction of these claims. As my aim is to find a way out of this apparent impasse, I am cautiously optimistic about receiving a fair hearing from those at the chalkface.

Perhaps I am wrong about how parents and teachers think about these matters. Perhaps most parents assume that they are entitled to pass on their moral standards by non-rational means, and most teachers assume that their role is to teach moral codes neutrally, and neither are inclined to question their assumptions. If so, my theory will turn out to be practitioner-unaligned and I shall find it harder than I am hoping to attract the attention of moral educators. That would be disappointing; but it would not affect the nature of the problem outlined in this chapter. Whether or not parents and teachers recognise the threat posed by reasonable moral disagreement is of secondary importance. What matters is that the threat is real, and unmitigated by any of the standard responses.

2

MORAL STANDARDS

In explaining the problem with which this book is concerned, I have made some assumptions about the nature of morality – or, at least, about a central and significant part of morality. In particular, I have assumed that morality involves both *subscribing to moral standards* and *believing them to be justified*. I shall now try to explain and justify these assumptions.

Subscription to standards

One of the things human beings do is hold themselves, and sometimes each other, to standards or norms of conduct. We follow rules, obey laws, adhere to principles and comply with policies. In some cases, such as New Year's resolutions, adoption of a standard is a deliberate and dateable event and adherence to it requires continual motivational effort and regular self-reminders of one's reasons for subscribing. In other cases, such as rules of subject–verb agreement in one's first language, adoption is a gradual and subconscious process and subsequent adherence comes quite naturally, without need of effort or reminders, and even without the ability to formulate the rules one is following. Typically, perhaps, if it is possible to generalise over such a large and diverse class, subscription to standards falls somewhere between these poles: the rules we follow in our day-to-day lives soon become second nature to us, so that compliance requires no special effort; but from time to time, when action contrary to our standards appears to promise some benefit or advantage, we find it helpful to remind ourselves, if not of our reasons for subscribing, then at least of the fact that we subscribe.

Standards come in many shapes and sizes. Some are trivial (pour the milk before the tea); others momentous (love the Lord your God with all your heart and with all your soul and with all your mind). Some are precise (exercise for thirty minutes three times a week); others vague (do the right thing). Some are specific to particular activities or contexts (drive on the left); others are quite general, applying to all activities in all contexts (live in the moment). Some are epistemic (proportion your beliefs to the evidence), some grammatical (don't split infinitives), some medical (take two tablets at bedtime), some horticultural (plant spring-flowering bulbs in the autumn).

Subscription to a standard is, to borrow David Copp's term, a 'syndrome' of attitudes and dispositions (Copp, 1995, p.85). It is at once conative, affective and behavioural. A person who subscribes to a standard characteristically intends to comply with it, feels good about complying with it and bad about failing to comply with it, and habitually does comply with it. Intentions, feelings and habits often line up in this way. Many people intend to exercise for thirty minutes three times a week, successfully stick to the regime, are pleased with themselves for sticking to it and feel guilty about taking a week off. Similarly, those charged with remembering to take medication at bedtime typically try to remember, do remember, are glad to have remembered and feel annoyed when they forget. These are pure or paradigmatic cases of subscription to a standard.

Sometimes intentions, feelings and habits do not line up so neatly. I may deliberately and routinely pour the milk before the tea, but feel neither good about compliance nor bad about non-compliance because the standard is not sufficiently important to me. I may have a habit of avoiding split infinitives in the absence of an intention to avoid them: perhaps I gave up the intention on hearing the arguments of grammarians for abandoning the rule, but have never managed to shake off the habit. And most of us make any number of New Year's resolutions that we intend to keep and feel bad about failing to keep, but that we never acquire anything resembling a tendency to keep. In these cases, where some but not all of the criteria for subscription are satisfied, we might prefer to speak of partial subscription, or of subscription in an attenuated sense.

Subscription to standards is conative, affective and behavioural, but it is not cognitive. It does not involve knowing, believing or judging that anything is the case. Standards are not, and do not entail, propositions, so subscription to them is not, and does not entail, assent to propositions. A standard, remarks Copp, is 'anything that is expressible by an imperative' (ibid., p.20), and it is in the semantics of imperatives that standards are at home:

> The notion of a standard is needed in the semantics of imperatival sentences that express commands, such as 'Shut the door'. Just as the corresponding indicative sentence expresses the proposition that you will shut the door, this sentence expresses the command (for you) *to* shut the door. The command specifies that the addressee is to shut the door, it is something the addressee can conform to and comply with, and it is not a proposition. Hence, it is a standard.
>
> *(ibid.)*

A standard specifies something to be done and the person who subscribes to it commits herself to doing the thing specified. Her commitment consists in a syndrome of intentions, feelings and habits, but not in a set of beliefs about the thing to be done or the reasons for doing it. She may have such beliefs, of course, and they may be related in important ways to her subscription to the standard, but they are not integral to it.

The idea of subscription to standards is, I hope, a familiar and intuitive one. We are rule-following creatures: all of us intentionally and habitually act in accordance with rules, norms and principles. And we frequently care enough about the rules we follow to take pride in complying with them and feel guilty about our failures to comply.

Believing standards to be justified

It always makes sense to ask of a standard to which one subscribes, or to which one is thinking about subscribing, whether subscription is justified. What counts as an adequate justification will be different for standards of different kinds. Where a standard is an arbitrary convention the function of which is to coordinate behaviour in a social group, for example, what justifies subscription to it is precisely the fact that it has currency in the group in question. I subscribe to the standard 'drive on the left' for the very good reason that everyone else in my country of residence subscribes to that standard too. By contrast, I subscribe to the standard 'plant spring-flowering bulbs in the autumn' because I know that spring-flowering bulbs require a sustained dormant period of cold temperatures to stimulate root development. Whether this horticultural standard happens to be current in a social group is quite irrelevant to the justification for subscribing to it.

Subscription to a given standard is either justified or unjustified. It either enjoys the support of a sound justificatory argument or it does not. If it does, and I am acquainted with and persuaded by the argument, I have a warranted belief that it is justified. If it does not, and I am acquainted with and persuaded by the sound objections to attempted justifications, I have a warranted belief that it is unjustified. If I find myself unable to assess the soundness of a justificatory argument, or I know there are attempted justifications I have yet to consider, it will be rational for me to remain agnostic about whether or not subscription to the standard is justified.

As with beliefs of other kinds, the beliefs people hold about the justificatory status of their standards are often unwarranted. Some people who favour pouring the milk before the tea base their practice on the false belief that cups are likely to crack on contact with very hot water. Others rely on some legitimate but weak consideration (one can save a little time by pouring the milk while the tea steeps in the pot), while culpably failing to notice the strong counter-consideration declared unanswerable by George Orwell: 'by putting the tea in first and stirring as one pours, one can exactly regulate the amount of milk, whereas one is liable to put in too much milk if one does it the other way round' (Orwell, 1946). In these cases, people believe without warrant that the milk-first standard is justified. And, importantly, their belief remains unwarranted even if it turns out that the milk-first standard *is* justified. Perhaps it is true, as some contend, that the tannin compounds in tea react differently with the casein in milk, in such a way as to affect the taste of the resulting drink, depending on whether the milk is poured first or last, and perhaps milk-first tea is generally more congenial to the human palate. If so, and if this is a weightier tea-making consideration than any other, there is a sound justification for the milk–first standard. But those who believe the standard to be justified on some other basis are still believing without warrant: it is just good luck that their unwarranted belief happens to be true.

This is, of course, a frivolous example. Tea-making standards are trivial, so unwarranted beliefs about their justificatory status hardly matter. But it is easy to think of standards for which unwarranted justificatory beliefs are more harmful. Consider the standard 'take two tablets at bedtime'. If one's reason for adhering to this standard is that the course of treatment has been prescribed by a trusted and qualified medical practitioner, all well and good. But suppose one adheres to it on the authority of a homeopath, or a herbalist, or an elderly relative convinced that the cure for every ailment is a daily dose of cod liver oil. In these cases one has no warrant for believing the standard to be justified, and the likely consequence of believing it is a steady worsening of the medical condition one is trying to treat.

Sometimes assessing the arguments for and against subscription to a standard is extraordinarily difficult. Much ink has been spilled over the last two or three millennia on the justificatory status of the standard 'love the Lord your God with all your heart and with all your soul and with all your mind'. Reasonable people continue to disagree about whether there is anything answering to the description 'the Lord your God' and, if there is, whether it is the sort of thing we have reason to love. Should we agree with Paley that the world bears sufficient resemblance to a watch to justify the inference to a cosmic watchmaker, or with Hume that it more closely resembles an animal or vegetable, so that 'its origin ought rather to be ascribed to generation or vegetation than to reason or design' (Hume, 1990 [1779], p.86)? If we accept some version of the design argument, are there grounds for positing one designer rather than several, or for supposing him to be an omnipotent creator rather than a cowboy builder who has 'botched and bungled [worlds] throughout an eternity, ere this system was struck out' (ibid., p.77)? Given the appalling suffering in the world, should we respond to its creator with wholehearted love, cautious deference or open hostility? If we are offered future harmony as compensation for present suffering, should we gratefully accept or follow Ivan Karamazov in giving back our entrance ticket, because 'too high a price is asked for harmony' (Dostoevsky, 2010 [1880], p.268)? And even if we have well-founded doubts about the existence or loveability of God, is it nevertheless prudent to make ourselves believe in and love him on the strength of Pascal's infamous wager: 'If you gain, you gain all; if you lose, you lose nothing' (Pascal, 2011 [1660], p.87)? These are questions with which one can wrestle for a lifetime without resolving to one's satisfaction.

While it always makes sense to ask whether subscription to a standard is justified, it does not follow that subscribers will always ask this question, or that they will care too much about the answer to it. It is quite possible, and quite common, for people to follow rules with great diligence and with no thought for the question of justification. Some wholehearted lovers of God simply do not trouble themselves with the thorny problems of his existence and loveability. Nor is it unusual for people to keep following rules even when they have carefully examined their reasons for doing so and found them wanting. Fideism is the familiar refuge of those who judge their religious commitments to be rationally indefensible but hold on to them anyway.

And just as we can adhere to a rule without believing adherence to be justified, so we can believe adherence to be justified without actually adhering. The world is not short of lotus-eaters who grasp and endorse the good reasons for exercising for thirty minutes three times a week, or of dogmatists who are convinced by the arguments for proportioning their beliefs to the evidence. The cognitive judgment that subscription to a standard is justified does not necessarily generate the conative, affective and behavioural dispositions that constitute subscription.

Problems arise when subscribing to a standard and believing subscription to be justified come apart like this. In the case of belief without subscription, we may find ourselves frustrated, disappointed or embarrassed by our failure to commit ourselves in practice to standards we endorse in principle. And in the case of subscription without belief, we are deprived of our best weapon against flagging resolve. As noted above, we bolster our determination to keep New Year's resolutions, or to comply with any other standard that requires resisting temptation or overcoming wayward desires, by issuing regular self-reminders of our reasons for subscribing. Moreover, regardless of whether this sort of determination-bolstering is needed, it is difficult to hold oneself to any standard indefinitely in the absence of some understanding of why one is doing so. Even the most incurious and pietistic lover of God is likely to stray from the narrow path eventually without some theological basis for her devotion. So the separation of subscribing to a standard and believing subscription to be justified is an infelicitous state of affairs; but that should not prevent us from acknowledging that it is a familiar and unexceptional feature of our lives.

Moral subscription to standards

That some of our standards are appropriately classified as *moral* standards is uncontroversial. Rather more controversial is the question of how the class of moral standards is to be delimited. I see little prospect of formulating a descriptive definition of this class that includes all the standards ordinarily described as 'moral' and excludes all the standards ordinarily not so described: ordinary usage here is too divergent, too elastic, too subject to interference from theoretical background noise. Instead I shall offer a stipulative definition that is, I think, intuitively plausible and broadly consonant with ordinary usage, and that helps to explain why disagreement about moral standards troubles us so much more than disagreement about standards of other kinds.

A person's moral standards have two distinguishing features. Both features have to do with the way she subscribes to the standards in question, rather than the form or content of the standards themselves. Any standard at all can be held as a moral standard, and the same standard can be moral for one person and non-moral for another. Content neutrality is advantageous in an account of moral standards precisely because it can accommodate the familiar distinction between moral and non-moral varieties of, say, vegetarianism or teetotalism. Moral and non-moral vegetarians alike subscribe to the standard 'don't eat meat', but they subscribe to it in importantly different ways.

The first distinguishing feature of moral subscription to standards is that the subscriber not only intends and inclines to comply with the standards in question, but also desires and expects everyone else to comply with them too. Sometimes we mind not at all whether others follow the same rules as we do; at other times we mind only that our rules have currency in a particular group to which we belong. Where our subscription to standards is a personal or local matter, the standards are not moral ones. It is only standards to which our subscription is universally-enlisting, in the sense that we want and expect everyone to comply with them, that are candidates for classification as moral.

It will be clear that subscription to standards like 'pour the milk before the tea', 'exercise for thirty minutes three times a week' and 'plant spring-flowering bulbs in the autumn' does not usually meet this first criterion of moral subscription. We may conscientiously hold ourselves to these standards, and we may have good reasons for doing so, but few of us are inclined to hold everyone else to them too. We may pity those who lack the good sense to comply with our tea-making or bulb-planting standards, but we rarely feel indignation at their non-compliance, or moved to campaign for the global currency of these standards. One does, occasionally, come across a health fanatic who feels so strongly about the benefits of an exercise regime that she takes active steps to enlist everyone else to her cause and is aggrieved by anyone's unwillingness to sign up: but this is just the point at which one becomes tempted to describe subscription to a health standard as moral.

By contrast, the way in which most of us subscribe to standards like 'do not lie' and 'do not steal' *is* universally-enlisting. Here it is not only our own compliance that matters to us, but everyone else's too. We expect others not to lie or steal, are dismayed when they do, and actively support the global currency of prohibitions on these forms of conduct. Whereas the culinary and horticultural practices of others are their own business, we see their lying and stealing as in some sense our business too. Of course our subscription to these standards does not *have* to be universally-enlisting: it is quite possible to hold oneself scrupulously to the prohibition on lying while caring not a jot about lies told by others. But someone who cares not a jot about lies told by others is not someone to whom lying is morally objectionable.

Moral subscription to standards, then, is universally-enlisting. Note that this definitional claim is quite different from the similar-looking justificatory claim that justified moral standards are universalisable. So far I have said nothing at all about what, if anything, might justify moral standards. For the moment I am only concerned with how moral standards differ from standards of other kinds. It is very plausible that universally-enlisting subscription to a standard could only be justified if the standard were universalisable: free-riders on the established practice of making and repaying loans may stand to gain by adhering to the maxim 'default on loans', but it would hardly be rational for them to want and expect everyone else to adhere to this maxim too. But universally-enlisting subscription to non-universalisable standards is perfectly *possible*, even if unjustified. A not-too-smart free-rider might sincerely want the loan-defaulting standard to have global currency, without noticing the consequences for the practice of making and repaying loans.

The second distinguishing feature of moral subscription to standards is an inclination to endorse penalties for non-compliance. Our moral standards are those whose violation we are ready to see punished in some way. To endorse a penalty for violation of a standard is to support the imposition of some deprivation or burden on the violator in response to their violation. People who fail to comply with our grammatical or epistemic norms may irritate or displease us, but we do not usually support their being punished. We may wince at Captain Kirk's five-year mission 'to boldly go where no man has gone before', but we do not invoke sanctions against screenwriters who recklessly split infinitives. In the case of thieves and liars, by contrast, our inclination to condemn or censure is strong. This penalty-endorsing criterion of moral subscription is famously noted by John Stuart Mill:

> For the truth is, that the idea of penal sanction, which is the essence of law, enters not only into the conception of justice, but into that of any kind of wrong. We do not call anything wrong, unless we mean to imply that a person ought to be punished in some way or other for doing it; if not by law, by the opinion of his fellow-creatures; if not by opinion, by the reproaches of his own conscience. This seems the real turning point of the distinction between morality and simple expediency ... [There are things] we wish that people should do, which we like or admire them for doing, perhaps dislike or despise them for not doing, but yet admit that they are not bound to do; it is not a case of moral obligation; we do not blame them, that is, we do not think that they are proper objects of punishment.
>
> *(Mill, 1962 [1861], pp.303–304)*

The penalties we endorse for non-compliance are not all of a piece. At one end of the spectrum are the sort of severe penalties by which offenders are deprived of their life (capital punishment), liberty (imprisonment) or wealth (fines). Such penalties are typically endorsed for non-compliance with prohibitions on conduct that causes significant harm to others (killing, violence, theft, etc.), and the mechanism for imposing them is usually a formal system of criminal law. At the other end of the spectrum are the sort of mild penalties by which offenders are made to feel uncomfortable or ashamed, such as rebukes, admonitions, tuts and frowns. These mild penalties are informal and spontaneous and may be seen as sufficient for offences like failing to keep a promise to a friend or failing to help someone in need (though they are also routinely imposed as supplements to more severe penalties). Between the two extremes lie many penalties of intermediate severity and formality, such as exclusion from an educational institution for cheating in an exam, termination of employment for sexual harassment, and ejection from a restaurant for drunk and disorderly behaviour. Different moral subscribers may favour penalties of different degrees of severity for non-compliance with the same standard; but the fact that they favour penalties of some kind is what makes their subscription moral.

A standard is moral, then, when a person's subscription to it is both universally-enlisting and penalty-endorsing; that is, when she wants and expects everyone to comply with it and supports some kind of punishment for non-compliance.[1] As noted above, this is a content neutral account of moral standards because any standard can be subscribed to in this way and the same standard can be moral for one person and non-moral for another. The difference between moral and non-moral vegetarians is that the former want everyone to refrain from eating meat, are distressed by the meat-eating of others and favour sanctions against meat-eaters, if only in the form of rebukes and admonitions. Non-moral vegetarians either do not mind about the meat-eating of others or are disinclined to condemn them for it.

Subscription to a standard can be universally-enlisting but not penalty-endorsing, and penalty-endorsing but not universally-enlisting. Still, it should not be surprising that the two features are often found together. If I expect everyone to comply with a standard, supporting penalties for non-compliance will be an obvious way to see that my expectation is met; and if non-compliance with a standard matters enough to me that I am ready to see it punished, there is a good chance it will matter to me regardless of who is failing to comply. So the two distinguishing features of moral subscription are natural bedfellows, even if they part company from time to time.

Having a tolerably clear account of what constitutes moral subscription does not, of course, imply that determining which cases of subscription qualify as moral will be straightforward. Sometimes our subscription to standards is only intermittently universally-enlisting and penalty-endorsing. Consider the person who subscribes unambiguously to the standard 'have one spouse at a time', but has mixed feelings about the polygamous practices of others. As far as her own conduct is concerned, she intends to comply with the monogamy standard, does in fact comply with it, and feels good about complying with it. Sometimes she is inclined to hold others to the monogamy standard too, feels disapproval of people in plural marriages, and favours legal sanctions against them. But at other times, in more liberal moods, she is inclined to live and let live, sees her choice to be monogamous as a personal matter, and wishes polygamists well in their alternative marital structure. Are we to say of such a person that her subscription to the standard 'have one spouse at a time' is moral? The question admits of no clear answer. And perhaps, in societies whose members are influenced by both conservative and liberal traditions of moral thought, cases of intermittent or wavering moral subscription will be rather common.

It should nevertheless be clear that all or most of us do in fact subscribe to at least some of our standards as moral standards. We are disposed not only to comply with prohibitions on killing, stealing, lying and cheating, but also to expect compliance of others and to sanction penalties for non-compliance. It should also be clear why disagreement about moral standards is so troubling to us: moral subscription is highly intrusive into the lives of others. Standards to which I hold myself alone are, in the main, my own business: it matters little to anyone else how I make my tea, keep myself fit or tend my garden. But standards to which I hold everyone, and which I am ready to see enforced by penalties for non-compliance, affect others very directly. You will not mind too much if I intend and incline to abide by a code of sexual conduct you find absurdly restrictive; but you will mind a great deal if I try to impose my restrictive code on you. It is the impositional character of moral subscription that makes moral disagreement so affronting, and so likely to cause conflict among the parties to the disagreement.

A standard to which my subscription is universally-enlisting and penalty-endorsing is one to which I am likely to hold myself with more-than-usual diligence. If my investment in a standard is such that I expect everyone to comply with it and I support penalties for non-compliance, the thought of violating it myself will tend to upset me more than the thought of violating other standards to which I subscribe. In this sense we might say that moral subscription is typically more stringent than non-moral subscription. And we might expect that, in most cases of conflict between a person's moral and non-moral standards, the former will trump the latter. But note that this is a weaker claim than the familiar proposal that overridingness is a necessary feature of moral standards. I see no reason to think that our subscription to standards is ever overriding, insofar as this implies that the standards in question invariably trump all others, so to make overridingness a criterion of moral subscription yields the unfortunate result that no one has moral standards. We frequently find ourselves in situations to which more than one of our many and diverse standards apply, and in which the applicable standards pull us in different directions; and while we may be generally inclined to prioritise some kinds of standard over others, there is none we are not sometimes prepared to violate if the countervailing inclinations are sufficiently strong. The conclusion to be drawn from this is not that morality is an illusion, but that it is a mistake to build into the definition of moral standards a lexical priority over standards of other kinds. Moral subscription is stringent, but not overriding.

Note, too, that the stringency with which we subscribe to our moral standards does not imply a preoccupation with them. We *may* be preoccupied with them if, for example, we find ourselves constantly tempted to violate them, or if we are mixing with people who flagrantly flout them. But where our subscription to moral standards is well entrenched and our compliance habitual, and where the standards have widespread currency in our society, we may ordinarily give them no more thought than we give to rules of subject–verb agreement. If I have acquired a strong and stable disinclination to steal, and I can take it for granted that others share my disinclination, there is no need for me to dwell or harp on the prohibition on stealing. I will still be dismayed when thefts occur, and will still support their being punished, but I will not spend much time contemplating or preaching their wickedness. Subscription to standards can be moral without being moralising.

Believing moral standards to be justified

As with standards of other kinds, it always makes sense to ask of one's moral standards whether subscription to them is justified. Moral subscription to a given standard either does or does not enjoy the support of a sound justificatory argument. If it does, and I am acquainted with and persuaded by the argument, I have a warranted belief that moral subscription is justified. If it does not, and I am acquainted with and persuaded by the sound objections to attempted justifications, I have a warranted belief that it is unjustified. And if I am unsure about the soundness of attempted justifications, it will be rational for me to remain agnostic about whether or not subscription is justified.

Is it, in fact, the case that some moral standards enjoy the support of a sound justificatory argument? That is a question on which much turns for the enterprise of moral education. If moral educators are charged with bringing it about that children subscribe to moral standards *and believe them to be justified*, they need to know whether the beliefs they are imparting are warranted and what that warrant looks like. The reasonable disagreement about morality described in the previous chapter poses a threat to moral education precisely because it suggests that warranted justificatory beliefs are unavailable in the moral sphere. I shall return to this pivotal question in later chapters; for the moment I will just observe that the two distinguishing features of moral subscription make hefty demands on a justificatory argument. Even if it were demonstrably and irrefutably true that milk-first tea tastes better, or that exercising for thirty minutes three times a week significantly improves health, these facts would scarcely entitle me to impose my tea-making and exercise-taking standards on everyone else. What a justification for moral subscription must show is not only that there is good reason for me to comply with a standard, but also that there is good reason for me to expect compliance of others and endorse penalties for non-compliance. This is plainly a taller justificatory order than we ordinarily have to fill for our non-moral standards.

Of course, people can, and do, ignore the question of justification. Again, in common with standards of other kinds, it is possible to subscribe to a moral standard without believing it to be justified, and to believe a moral standard to be justified without subscribing to it. For an example of the former, think of the way some people disapprove of same-sex relationships and condemn those who enter into them, yet openly admit that they can give no reason for their disapproval. For an example of the latter, think of the person who is intellectually persuaded by the moral arguments for vegetarianism but finds herself unwilling either to give up meat herself or to castigate others for not doing so. It may be that the phenomenon of misalignment between the standards to which people subscribe and the justificatory beliefs they hold is actually more prevalent in the area of morality than elsewhere. Because our moral dispositions are often formed in early childhood, and because we soon become aware of reasonable disagreement about the content and justification of morality, complete congruence between moral standards and justificatory beliefs may be the exception rather than the rule.

If the phenomenon of misalignment is more prevalent in the area of morality, it is also more infelicitous. In the case of belief without subscription, our failure to commit ourselves to standards we consider important enough to merit penalties for non-compliance may induce in us something closer to shame or humiliation than frustration or embarrassment. Judging that exercise would be good for us but failing to take it is one thing; judging that meat is murder but continuing to eat it is quite another. And in the case of subscription without belief, the loss of our best weapon against flagging resolve will be most sorely felt when it is our moral standards we are tempted to violate. Moral violations, because of our inclination to punish ourselves for them, cost us more than non-moral violations (irrespective of their cost to others), so we have a particular interest in being able to bolster our determination to comply by reminding ourselves of our reasons for doing so. Moreover, while it is sometimes the case that moral compliance is so entrenched and habitual among the members of a social group that determination-bolstering is unnecessary, this should not obscure the fact that we are often sorely tempted to do the things our standards prohibit, and highly reluctant to do the things our standards require. In many situations it is to our immediate advantage to break a promise, tell a lie, take what does not belong to us or disregard the interests of another. Conflicts between the lure of advantage and the demands of morality prompt us to question the latter, to look for ways of circumventing or discounting them. If we can reassure ourselves that our dispositions to refrain from promise-breaking, lying and stealing are not pathological barriers to the satisfaction of our desires, but rather justified constraints on our freedom of action, we can strengthen our resolve to conduct ourselves accordingly. There are no guarantees, of course: the lure of advantage is sometimes irresistible, even for someone whose moral determination to resist it is bolstered by justificatory beliefs; but those without such beliefs are significantly more vulnerable to this sort of temptation.

Perhaps it will be countered that, in areas where justifying subscription to standards is unduly difficult, there may actually be some advantage to subscribers in giving the question of justification a wide berth. The point is familiar enough in relation to religious standards like 'love the Lord your God with all your heart and with all your soul and with all your mind'. Wholehearted lovers of God who decline to engage with the questions of God's existence and loveability may be saving themselves a good deal of metaphysical perplexity and existential anxiety. If the difficulty of justifying moral standards is comparable to the difficulty of justifying religious ones, might it not be sensible for moral agents to give up the idea of having good reasons for their standards? Might not religious and moral standards be easier to hold on to if one refuses to be drawn into theological and moral-philosophical inquiries?

This line of thought is not to be lightly dismissed. It does not count against the claim that subscription without belief is infelicitous in the ways I have indicated; rather it moots the possibility that the cost of not having justificatory beliefs is more than compensated for by the gain of not having to contend with the business of justification. How seriously this possibility deserves to be taken in the moral sphere depends on just how difficult it is to justify moral standards.

I shall say of a person who both subscribes to a moral standard and believes it to be justified that she is *fully committed* to it. Someone is fully committed to a moral standard when she intends and inclines to comply with it, wants and expects everyone else to comply with it, and endorses penalties for non-compliance, *and* when she thinks she has good reason for intending, expecting and endorsing these things.

A note on terminology. The phrase 'belief that subscription to a moral standard is justified' is cumbersome and it is tempting to abbreviate it to 'moral belief'. I am going to resist this temptation. To hold a moral belief, it is widely supposed, is to assent to the propositional content of an indicative sentence that predicates moral rightness or wrongness of a specified form of conduct ('cheating is wrong'), or moral duty or obligation of specified or unspecified persons ('you ought to keep your promises'). But it is notoriously controversial that indicative sentences of this kind *have* propositional content. And among those who think they do, it is further controversial that the propositions in question are claims about the justification of subscription to moral standards. As the foregoing account of moral standards and justificatory beliefs is neutral on these points, it seems to me sensible to avoid the term 'moral belief'.

Moral non-cognitivists argue that someone who utters the indicative sentence 'cheating is wrong' is not asserting that some state of affairs obtains, but rather issuing a prescription ('do not cheat'), expressing an attitude of disapproval ('boo to cheating') or performing an act of condemnation ('I hereby condemn you for cheating'). Perhaps they are right about this. Certainly those whose subscription to selected standards is universally-enlisting and penalty-endorsing will be in the business of issuing prescriptions, expressing disapproval and performing condemnations. It may be that locutions of the form 'X is right/wrong' and 'One ought/ought not to X' are properly understood as the tools of this trade. As long as the non-cognitivist is prepared to allow that it makes sense to ask whether universally-enlisting and penalty-endorsing subscription is justified, there is no need to challenge her view that there are no moral propositions and therefore no moral beliefs.

Moral cognitivists think that indicative moral sentences do have propositional content. A cognitivist might hold, for example, that 'cheating is wrong' attributes the metaphysically queer property of wrongness to acts of cheating. She might further hold that there is no such thing as the property of wrongness: that is, she might be an error theorist who takes the view that all moral propositions are false and all moral beliefs unwarranted. Again, provided she admits the possibility of distinguishing between good reasons and bad reasons for subscribing to moral standards, her error theory about moral propositions need not concern us.

Of course, moral cognitivists *can* think that the propositions expressed by indicative moral sentences are, in fact, propositions about the justificatory status of moral standards. Here, 'cheating is wrong' means, roughly, 'moral subscription to a prohibition on cheating is justified'. David Copp, on whose account of moral standards I have drawn heavily in this chapter, defends a position along these lines. He writes:

the sentences we use to make normative claims express *propositions* about relevant *standards*. In central or paradigmatic cases, the proposition expressed by a *moral* claim entails that some relevant *moral* standard is justified. This is so in virtue of the truth conditions or content of the proposition expressed.

(Copp, 1995, p.10)

Copp's 'standard-based theory' of the truth conditions of normative propositions is attractive and plausible, but it is not demonstrably true. If it were, I should have no hesitation in abbreviating 'belief that subscription to a moral standard is justified' to 'moral belief'. But because there persists deep and reasonable disagreement about the existence and nature of moral beliefs, I shall stick to the more cumbersome formulation.

Ethical standards

Finally, let me introduce a distinction between moral standards and ethical ones. Following Bernard Williams (1985), I take the domain of ethics to be delimited by the scope of 'Socrates' question': how should one live? This question, as Williams notes, is *general*, in being concerned with what it is for anyone to live well, and *holistic*, in being concerned with how one should think about life as a whole. The aim of ethical inquiry, then, is to say something sensible about the kinds of human life that are most worth living – and by extension about the kinds that are not worth living.

Ethical inquiries may or may not yield the conclusion that living well consists, in part, in holding oneself to certain standards of conduct. Insofar as it does yield this conclusion, the standards in question are ethical ones. My ethical standards are those to which I subscribe on the grounds that I consider them integral to a life worth living. Note that this ties ethical standards to a particular kind of justificatory belief: a standard to which I adhere without reason, or to whose justification I have given no thought, will not qualify as ethical.

Ethical standards are sometimes but not always moral, and moral standards are sometimes but not always ethical. If a person has a set of standards she judges to be integral to a life worth living, and also a set of standards to which her subscription is universally-enlisting and penalty-endorsing, there is a good chance that the two sets will overlap. Believing a standard to be necessary for human flourishing may fuel a desire to enlist others to it, and feeling strongly enough about a standard to favour penalties for non-compliance may connect with the thought that people cannot live well without it. But there is no necessity about this overlap, and it will rarely be complete. The reasons people have for moral subscription need not be ethical; indeed, as we have seen, they need not have reasons at all. People who disapprove of same-sex relationships and condemn those who enter into them, in the absence of any justificatory belief, have a moral standard that prohibits same-sex relationships but not an ethical one. By the same token, one may have perfectly good ethical reasons for subscribing to a standard without feeling any inclination to impose it on everyone else. Someone fully persuaded that only an examined life is worth living may be quite unwilling to demand self-examination of others, let alone to see them punished for leading unexamined lives.

It is important to recognise that non-moral subscription to ethical standards does not represent a failure of nerve, a regrettable reluctance to throw one's full conative weight behind one's considered ethical judgments. To the contrary, there is no reason to think that ethical justifications for subscription to standards will generally serve as justifications for *moral* subscription to standards. My sincere, reflective judgment that only an examined life is worth living gives me good grounds for holding myself to a standard of self-examination, but no grounds at all for holding everyone else to it. My chosen ethical standard might seem to me worth shouting about, worth presenting to others for their consideration, but by what right could I impose it on them? And, if I endorse penalties for others' non-compliance with my ethical standards, by what right could I object to being penalised for non-compliance with theirs?

Ethical standards, then, differ from moral standards in being distinguished by the reasons one has for subscribing, rather than by the way one subscribes. And, crucially, the reasons for subscribing that make a standard ethical are not, in and of themselves, the kind of reasons one would need to justify moral subscription.

Note

1   This account of moral standards is heavily indebted to, though not quite the same as, the one advanced by David Copp in his *Morality, Normativity and Society* (Copp, 1995).

3

TWO KINDS OF MORAL EDUCATION

Moral education is education in or about morality. Morality is, in whole or in part, a matter of subscribing to moral standards and believing them to be justified. So moral education is, in whole or in part, education in or about this matter.

I leave open the question of whether there is more to morality, and hence more to moral education, than moral standards and justificatory beliefs. Perhaps there is. There may, for example, be certain conative and affective dispositions that are not well understood as inclinations to comply with standards, but that are appropriately described as 'moral' and are capable of being cultivated by educators. Some of the dispositions traditionally designated 'virtues' may fall into this category. It is plausible to think of virtues as moderating basic human emotions and motivations, rather than regulating conduct directly. Courage, on this view, is not a disposition to perform or refrain from performing a specified type of action; it is a disposition to be neither paralysed by fear nor oblivious to it, to feel proportionate, non-debilitating and action-motivating levels of fear. If virtues differ from inclinations to comply with standards, and if it makes sense to classify some of them as moral, then moral standards and justificatory beliefs do not exhaust the range of moral phenomena.

It is not necessary for me to pronounce on this question. If there is more to morality than standards of conduct, the theory of moral education set out in this book will be, more precisely, a theory of a central and significant part of moral education. If not, it will be a theory of moral education in toto. I do not mind which of these it is taken to be.

In this chapter I shall argue for a distinction between two kinds of moral education, corresponding to the distinction between subscribing to moral standards and believing them to be justified. One thing moral educators might try to do is cultivate in children the conative, affective and behavioural dispositions that constitute subscription to moral standards. Another thing they might try to do is impart beliefs, or facilitate the formation of beliefs, about the justificatory status of moral standards. I will call these two endeavours *moral formation* and *moral inquiry* respectively.

Let me emphasise at the outset that the point of distinguishing these two kinds of moral education is not to suggest that they ought to be separated in practice. It is quite possible, and indeed quite normal, for moral formation and moral inquiry to be pursued in tandem and in ways that are at least intended to be mutually reinforcing. It is nevertheless important to understand that the two endeavours are logically distinct, and that each can be intelligibly pursued in the absence of the other.

Moral formation

We often think of education in largely cognitive terms. We think of it as a matter of imparting knowledge and understanding, of bringing it about that children hold the right beliefs for the right reasons, of equipping children with the ability to acquire information, evaluate claims, draw inferences and discern truths. While education is certainly concerned with these things, they do not exhaust its concerns. People learn, and are enabled by others to learn, not just what and how to think, but what and how to want, feel, do and be. The cognitive part of the soul is not the only part that is educable.

It is these other educable parts of the soul on which educators must work if they wish to bring it about that children subscribe to moral standards. Recall that a person who subscribes to a standard characteristically intends to comply with it, feels good about complying with it and bad about failing to comply with it, and habitually does comply with it. If her subscription to the standard is moral, she additionally wants and expects others to comply with it and endorses penalties for non-compliance. This syndrome of attitudes and dispositions can be deliberately cultivated in children, but not, or not primarily, by the expository and discursive methods ordinarily used to develop their knowledge and understanding.

What, then, does moral formation look like? I will briefly sketch what I take to be its principal methods, with the caveat that the following list is intended to be neither exhaustive nor prescriptive. I do not claim that these are the only ways in which children are brought to subscribe to moral standards; nor do I present the list as a recipe to be followed. My aim is simply to lay out and distinguish between the dominant methods by which parents and teachers do in fact cultivate moral attitudes and dispositions in children.

The first and most basic method of moral formation is the *issuing of prescriptions*. One way in which children learn not to do morally prohibited things is by being told not to do them. Imperatives such 'Don't hit your brother', 'Don't lie to me' and 'Don't take things that aren't yours' feature prominently in the lives of most children and play a foundational role in establishing habitual compliance with moral standards. Of course, children do not always follow rules and do not always defer to the authority of parents and teachers; but very often they *do* follow rules and defer to authority, and the more they follow an oft-repeated rule, the more habitual their rule-following becomes.

The ability to hold oneself to standards of conduct is rooted in the experience of being held to standards of conduct by others. The child's spontaneous, unregulated activity is interrupted by the issuance of a prescription to do something she would prefer not to, or to refrain from doing something she wants to do. She elects to comply with the prescription rather than indulge her desires; she allows her conduct to be regulated by the prescriber. This submission to regulation by others sets the template for subsequent self-regulation. Through the experience of having certain desires repeatedly thwarted by parental prescriptions not to act on them, the child learns to thwart her wayward desires for herself. She learns to self-prescribe and to give her self-prescriptions greater weight than her spontaneous inclinations and preferences. The ability to regulate one's conduct in this way is the fundamental moral capacity.

Prescriptions issued by parents and teachers need not, of course, be expressed in the imperative mood. There are perfectly serviceable indicative and interrogative alternatives. The prescriptions expressed by the imperatives above are just as well expressed by 'You shouldn't hit your brother', 'How dare you lie to me?' and 'It's wrong to take things that aren't yours'. Whatever view one takes on the propositional content of indicative moral sentences (and, for the reasons given in the previous chapter, I take no stand on this), it is plain that, in many practical contexts, they are intended by the speaker and understood by the listener to express prescriptions. The child who, poised to leave a neighbour's house with a pocketful of pilfered jewellery, hears the words 'It's wrong to take things that aren't yours' is not usually in any doubt that she is receiving an instruction, whatever else she may take those words to convey.

The issuing of moral prescriptions, ubiquitous in early childhood, becomes steadily less effective as children get older. As children take responsibility for the regulation of their own conduct, they become less receptive to the regulation of their conduct by others. Moreover, while young children frequently need to be reminded of the moral rules that bear on the actions they are contemplating, older children's non-compliance with moral rules is much less likely to be attributable to the absence of timely reminders. Unless their early moral formation has been seriously deficient, by the time children reach secondary school they know quite well, and have no trouble bringing to mind at the appropriate times, the standards by which they are supposed to regulate their conduct; if they fail to do so, it is because they are insufficiently impressed by the authority of the standards, or insufficiently worried by the consequences of non-compliance. And these insufficiencies will rarely be made good by reiteration of what the standards require.

Still, moral injunction and exhortation are not always out of place in the education of older children. A teacher investigating the causes of a playground fight may instruct those involved to tell her the truth, not because she thinks they will fail to recall this moral requirement, or because she thinks they are inveterate liars, but because she recognises that this is a situation in which the brawlers may be strongly motivated to lie, and in which she can assist them in attending to the voice of conscience by turning up its volume a little. The judicious use of external prescription to supplement and enhance the self-prescription of developing moral agents is entirely appropriate in the moral formation of adolescents.

A second method of moral formation is the *rewarding of compliance*. An important feature of subscription to a standard is feeling good about complying with it, and rewarding compliance helps to establish this affective association. The rewards most commonly used here are expressions of approval: compliments, commendations, thanks and smiles. While children are still learning the parameters of morally acceptable behaviour, rewarding compliance is a natural correlate of issuing pre-scriptions: children are first told what they are required to do, then warmly praised for doing it. In this way they learn not only to self-prescribe but also to self-reward, to give themselves a metaphorical pat on the back for successfully regulating their conduct.

Of course, many moral standards are such that compliance with them is not ordinarily praiseworthy. People are not usually congratulated for making it home from the shops without having stolen anything, or getting through a difficult conversation without throwing a punch. But for the moral novice who has not yet mastered her impulses, whose natural inclination is to take what she wants or lash out at those who annoy her, compliance with moral prohibitions on theft and vio-lence represents a real achievement, and rewarding it with expressions of approval both recognises the achievement and strengthens the inclination to comply.

And compliance with moral standards is sometimes praiseworthy even for those whose subscription to them is well established. When grievously provoked, it can be a challenge for moral agents at any stage of development to rein in their violent impulses – and grievous provocation is hardly an uncommon feature of adolescent lives. Sometimes we commend a young person's moral conduct not because it is commendable for a moral novice, but because it is commendable simpliciter. Here again the pedagogical function of the commendation is to reinforce the tendency to feel good about the conduct in question.

A third method, the flipside of the second, is the *punishing of non-compliance*. Just as rewarding compliance builds an association with positive affect and strengthens the inclination to comply, so punishing non-compliance builds an association with nega-tive affect and reduces the inclination not to comply. As children learn to self-reward from the experience of being praised for doing right, so they learn to self-punish from the experience of being told off for doing wrong. In these respects the two methods play parallel roles in the process of moral formation.

But their roles are not exactly parallel because of the special importance of punishment in moral life. Moral compliance, though routinely rewarded in young children, is only occasionally seen as praiseworthy in adults; moral non-compliance, by contrast, is always seen as deserving of punishment: this is just what is meant by the claim that moral subscription is penalty-endorsing. Because we expect others to conduct themselves in accordance with the requirements of morality, their doing so is not normally a cause for rejoicing; but their failing to do so is invariably a cause for disappointment or displeasure. So while praising children for doing right and telling them off for doing wrong both serve to establish affective associations, the point of the latter is also to instil an ongoing expectation of punishment for wrongdoing.

As noted in Chapter Two, the range of penalties we endorse for non-compliance with moral standards is wide, from tuts and frowns at one end of the spectrum to fines and imprisonment at the other. In the context of moral formation, the penalties imposed are in some respects less severe and in other respects more severe than those imposed in the course of ordinary moral life. Because children are not yet fully responsible for their actions, and because it would be impractical or developmentally harmful to put them through certain kinds of hardship, we exempt them, as far as possible, from the more serious penalties for moral non-compliance. But because punishments meted out to children have an expressly pedagogical purpose, they often take an exaggerated form. Expressions of disapproval are frequently more pronounced, and more public, when the misdeeds that prompt them are perpetrated by children. On learning that a friend has deceived me, I may take her to one side and quietly convey my disappointment; on learning that a pupil in my class has deceived me similarly, I may put on a display of outrage that far exceeds the displeasure I feel, and that is intended to cause a measure of public embarrassment. One reason for reacting differently in these cases is that I assume my friend is already feeling bad about the deception, whereas the pupil must be brought to feel bad by the severity of my response.

The three methods of moral formation so far considered – issuing prescriptions, rewarding compliance and punishing non-compliance – are what we might call direct methods. They are direct interventions into the practical lives of children, usually just before or just after they act in morally required or prohibited ways. These direct methods are characteristically accompanied by indirect ones, by attempts to shape children's intentions, feelings and habits through example and modelling rather than instruction and conditioning.

One such indirect method is the *modelling of compliance*. Children learn how to behave by watching the behaviour of others. If they observe their parents and teachers conducting themselves in morally compliant ways, they are more likely to be morally compliant themselves. Consider the moral requirement to help those in need, at least when doing so is not unduly burdensome to the helper. Children who see the adults in their lives devote time and effort to assisting people in trouble, distress, poverty or ill-health, who regularly witness compliance with the requirement to help those in need, tend to acquire the inclination to comply with it themselves. Children who rarely or never see this, while they may be sensitive to and upset by the suffering of others, are much less likely to feel a responsibility to do something about it.

The efficacy of compliance-modelling does not depend on parents and teachers having the status of role models. An adult is properly said to be a role model for a child when the child admires her and aspires to be like her. It is not uncommon for children, especially young children, to view their parents and teachers in exactly this light; and being admired is by no means a hindrance to the modelling of compliance. But nor is it a precondition for it. Learning that disagreements are not to be settled by violence and intimidation is in part a matter of routine exposure to situations in which disagreements are settled by negotiation and compromise, in which no-one resorts to aggressive or threatening behaviour. The point of this exposure is not so much to set before children an ideal to which they can aspire as to show them what is normally expected. It is the means by which children are brought to see that resolving conflicts peacefully is the way things are done around here. Children need not *admire* the adults who model compliance with moral standards, or aspire to be like them; they need only recognise them as people who know how to behave.

Another indirect method of moral formation is the *modelling of reactions to the compliance and non-compliance of others*. This is the third party analogue of rewarding compliance and punishing non-compliance. We reward and punish children for their good deeds and wrongdoings, but we also model for them positive and negative reactions to the good deeds and wrongdoings of others. We make sure they see us reprimanding their classmates for bullying, praising their siblings for telling the truth, expressing indignation at corruption in politics, and lauding international aid initiatives. By emulating the reactions we model, children become more inclined to feel and express approval of compliance and disapproval of non-compliance in the conduct of others.

One reason for encouraging these reactions to the compliance and non-compliance of others is simply that they reinforce children's own tendency to comply. A child who disapproves of a classmate's bullying is less likely to be a bully herself; and one who admires a sibling's honesty is more likely to tell the truth. There is a tight connection between how we feel about the things done by others and how we feel about the idea of doing those things ourselves.

But this is not the only reason for cultivating attitudes of approval and dis-approval in children. Subscription to moral standards is not just a matter of intending and inclining to comply; it is also a matter of wanting and expecting everyone else to comply. Moral formation must bring it about that children are both morally compliant themselves and ready to support the moral compliance of others. A lively concern for the beam in one's own eye ought not to eclipse con-cern for the mote in one's brother's. And the principal mechanism by which moral agents police each other's conduct is by responding positively to compliance and negatively to non-compliance. Teaching children to make these positive and negative responses, in appropriate ways at appropriate times, is achieved in large part by modelling them.

When a teacher publicly reprimands a playground bully, she is showing the rest of the class not just how to feel about bullying, but how to punish it. She is encouraging them, and equipping them with a form of words, to reprimand play-ground bullies for themselves. And by adjusting the severity of her public rebukes to the seriousness of the misdemeanour − a disappointed shake of the head for 'the dog ate my homework', a lengthy harangue for wilful damage to school property − she teaches her pupils to be proportionate in their expressions of disapproval, to develop a sense of the punishment that fits the crime.

These, then, are the chief methods by which parents and teachers bring it about that children subscribe to moral standards. By issuing prescriptions, rewarding compliance, punishing non-compliance, modelling compliance, and modelling reactions to the compliance and non-compliance of others, moral educators cultivate the syndrome of intentions, feelings and habits in which moral subscription consists.

I have emphasised that subscription to standards is conative, affective and behavioural but not cognitive. It does not, in and of itself, involve knowing, believing or judging that anything is the case. This is not to deny, of course, that people who subscribe to moral standards sometimes have to think, and think quite hard, about how to apply them. It is one thing to intend and incline to help those in need, another to work out, in any given context, whether the standard applies and what action it requires. A person can be in difficulty without being in need of help; and if she does need help, is it the kind that removes the burden from her shoulders or the kind that gives her the strength to bear it?

While the principal task of moral formation is the cultivation of subscription to moral standards by the methods just described, there is therefore a secondary task of improving children's thinking about the application of their standards. Here the appropriate teaching methods are the expository and discursive ones used to develop thinking in other areas of the school curriculum. Discussion, in particular, about how to meet one's moral obligations in specified circumstances, both real and hypothetical, is central to enhancing children's deliberative capacities. By thinking out loud, in dialogue with others, about what they ought or ought not to do in morally challenging situations, children learn to negotiate the subtleties and complexities of moral life.

Moral deliberation is needed when it is not immediately clear what morality requires. From the fact that it is not immediately clear to a moral agent – especially a novice moral agent – what morality requires, it does not follow that there is no clear answer available. Often it just takes a little time and thought to work through the options one is considering and the moral standards that bear on them. Suppose, for example, a young person is initially unsure about the permissibility of making a cruel joke at the expense of an unpopular classmate on a social media website. She sincerely subscribes to the moral prohibition on bullying and would not dream of physically hurting her classmate, or taking her dinner money, or even standing by while others hurt or took from her. But she does not immediately recognise jokes on social media sites as one of the forms bullying can take. There is no doubt that the course of action she is contemplating is, in fact, ruled out by the moral prohibition on bullying, but to see this she needs to think through what it is to bully someone and the nature of social media interaction.

Of course, it is sometimes the case that clear answers are not available. Moral deliberation does not always yield a decisive verdict on what morality requires. Recall the two kinds of reasonable disagreement about the application of moral standards identified in Chapter One, arising from conflicting moral demands and borderline cases of morally regulated actions. Such disagreements are reasonable precisely because careful thinking does not settle them. In cases where one must choose between telling the truth and sparing others pain, and where the truth matters and the anticipated pain is great, moral agents may reflect deeply and diligently and still disagree about the right course of action. And in the case of my holding on to books lent to me long ago in the expectation that they would be returned, which meets some but not all of the criteria used to identify instances of theft, neither clarifying the concept of theft nor inquiring further into the details of the case is likely to yield agreement on whether I have done wrong.

The unavailability of clear answers in these cases does not deprive deliberation of its point. The decisions moral agents make when confronted with conflicting moral demands or borderline cases of morally regulated actions matter a great deal, both to the agents themselves and to those affected by their decisions. Whichever way one jumps in a forced choice between telling the truth and sparing others pain, one must be able to live with the choice – and perhaps be able to justify it to those one hurts or deceives. Even where an agent knows in advance that deliberating will not yield an uncontroversially right course of action, she will still want to ensure that she has paid close attention to her options and the moral standards that bear on them (or might be thought to bear on them), and that her decision about what to do is as considered and as sensitive to moral constraints as circumstances permit.

It is therefore important that children and young people are given opportunities to think and talk about the application of their moral standards. They must acquire, in addition to moral intentions, feelings and habits, the ability to work through moral uncertainty and to cope with morally ambiguous situations. This cognitive aspect of moral formation is a necessary supplement to the central task of cultivating subscription to moral standards.

Its importance should not, however, be exaggerated. Moral deliberation is needed when it is not immediately clear what morality requires; but in the over-whelming majority of cases to which moral standards apply, what they require is obvious. There is usually no mystery at all about whether a specified course of action is a case of stealing, bullying, lying or cheating, and no room for uncertainty about whether or not morality permits it. Given the universally-enlisting and penalty-endorsing character of moral standards, it would be odd if they were generally difficult to apply. In many of the everyday contexts in which people are expected, on pain of punishment, to comply with moral standards, it would be hopelessly impractical to take time out to deliberate about what they require; if such delib-eration were routinely necessary, punishing non-compliance would be most unfair. Something has gone badly awry with a moral code if those who subscribe to it struggle to see what it requires of them. Moral dilemmas and borderline cases of morally regulated actions certainly crop up in the course of moral life, but they are the exception, not the rule. So learning to deliberate about the application of moral standards, necessary though it is, plays only a supporting role in the moral formation of children.

There is, moreover, a danger attendant on overemphasising the cognitive aspect of moral formation. Disproportionate attention to moral dilemmas and borderline cases can give children the quite misleading impression that moral standards are peculiarly difficult to apply. It can blur the line between knowing that people sometimes reasonably disagree about what their moral code requires and supposing that such disagreements are the norm. If, for example, a school were to address the topic of morality exclusively through discussion of intractable moral dilemmas, it would not be surprising if pupils came to think of moral standards as rules that characteristically conflict with each other, or are dauntingly difficult to follow. For obvious reasons, such misconceptions tend to undermine, rather than support, the attempt to bring it about that children subscribe to moral standards.

Moral inquiry

The second of the two kinds of moral education I wish to distinguish in this chapter is moral inquiry, by which I mean inquiry into the justificatory status of moral standards. I have suggested that, for a person to be fully committed to a moral standard, she must both subscribe to it and believe it to be justified. Moral inquiry is the part of moral education that attends to the latter component of full moral commitment.

Moral inquiry is straightforwardly cognitive. It is a matter of investigating the nature of moral standards, asking how subscription to such standards might be justified, and examining the strength of suggested justifications. It is logically quite distinct from the enterprise of cultivating subscription to moral standards: holding a belief about the justificatory status of a moral standard is neither a necessary nor a sufficient condition of subscribing to it. A child from a puritanical home might be brought to see, by force of rational argument, that there is no justification for a moral prohibition on masturbation, yet continue to find the thought of masturbation shameful, resist the temptation to do it, and disapprove of those who succumb to the temptation.

Moral inquiry is also logically distinct from the cognitive aspect of moral formation just discussed. Those who subscribe to moral standards must develop the deliberative capacity to cope with situations in which it is not immediately clear what their standards require. But deliberation about the application of moral standards is a different sort of undertaking from inquiry into their justification. It is one thing to be able to work out that cruel jokes on social media sites are ruled out by the prohibition on bullying, quite another to understand why bullying is prohibited in the first place.

Sometimes, when a parent or teacher engages a child in discussion about the justification of a moral standard, she does so with the aim of persuading the child that the standard is, or is not, justified. I shall call teaching with this aim *directive* moral inquiry. Deliberate attempts to persuade children that a prohibition on bullying is justified, or that a prohibition on masturbation is unjustified, are cases of directive moral inquiry. At other times, when a parent or teacher engages a child in discussion about the justification of a moral standard, she has no persuasive aim: her teaching is neutral or noncommittal with respect to the standard's justificatory status. I shall call teaching of this kind *nondirective* moral inquiry.

Consider two teachers, Dawn and Tim, exploring with their respective classes the question of whether there is a justified moral requirement to vote in general elections. As it happens, both teachers hold the view that there is such a requirement. They each introduce the topic by screening a television debate between asserters and deniers of a moral obligation to vote, then invite their classes to discuss the issue. In her chairing of the class discussion, Dawn opts to remain strictly neutral. She intervenes to maintain order, to ensure that everyone has an opportunity to speak, to request clarifications and to keep the discussion on track; but she makes no attempt to persuade her pupils of (what she takes to be) the correct view. Tim, by contrast, opts to steer the class discussion, gently and tactfully, towards the conclusion that voting is morally required. He ensures that (what he takes to be) the sound arguments for the requirement, and the sound objections to arguments against it, are thoroughly aired and understood, either by giving the floor to pupils able to articulate them or by feeding them into the discussion himself. He does not openly declare his view, and does nothing that could be construed as putting pressure on pupils to adopt his view: he merely guides the course of the discussion in such a way as to give due prominence to the strongest arguments.

Tim's teaching is directive and Dawn's nondirective. I make no comment here on which of these approaches to teaching the morality of voting is to be preferred. Rather I give the example to illustrate two points about the distinction between directive and nondirective moral inquiry.

First, the choice between directive and nondirective aims is not a choice between didactic and nondidactic methods. To teach didactically is to tell pupils how things are, to instruct, inform, expound or explain; to teach nondidactically is to provide opportunities for pupils to work out for themselves how things are, through exploration, investigation, discussion or play. Good teaching typically involves a judicious combination of didactic and nondidactic methods, and the optimum balance between them depends in part on the topic being taught. There are obvious practical reasons for relying more heavily on teacher exposition in a lesson on deep-sea biology than a lesson on conservation of volume. But the decision to teach a question directively rather than nondirectively carries no implication that didactic methods will be favoured over nondidactic ones.

Dawn and Tim both opt to use a nondidactic method – exploratory class discussion – to tackle the question of a moral obligation to vote. Neither attempts to tell pupils how things are: they do not offer instruction and they do not declare their own views. They each want their pupils to think through the morality of voting for themselves. The difference between them is that Tim has an aim Dawn does not have: the aim of bringing it about that his pupils come to one conclusion rather than another. Their different aims certainly affect what they do in the classroom (Tim exercises the prerogative of the chair to select and interject in ways that Dawn does not), but the things they do differently do not alter that fact that they are both teaching nondidactically.

Second, a teacher's decision about whether or not to teach a claim directively does not turn simply on whether or not she believes the claim. That there is a difference between what one believes and what one is entitled to persuade children to believe is perhaps most immediately apparent in the domain of religious education. In the UK, where all children receive religious education throughout their compulsory schooling (unless withdrawn by their parents), it is widely accepted that religious education teachers with sincerely held religious beliefs should not teach with the aim of bringing pupils to share those beliefs. Exactly why they should not do this is a matter of some dispute, but one plausible reason is that we operate with different evidential standards for adopting beliefs and imparting them to children. Where I recognise that a matter is not settled by the available evidence and argument, it may nevertheless strike me that one view on the matter is better supported than others and that committing myself to some view or other is preferable to reserving judgment. In these circumstances, it may be reasonable for me to adopt the better supported view but unreasonable for me to try to persuade children to adopt it.

In the Dawn and Tim example, both teachers believe there is a justified moral requirement to vote. But only one is prepared to steer pupils towards that conclusion. This may be because the two teachers make different assessments of the warrant for their belief. Tim thinks there are decisive reasons for believing the moral standard to be justified and aims to ensure that these reasons come to light in the course of class discussion. Dawn doubts that the reasons are decisive. Although she thinks her view is defensible, she sees the matter as one on which reasonable people reasonably disagree. So it seems to her inappropriate to teach with the aim of persuading her pupils that the standard is justified.

While it is easy enough to think of cases in which a matter is taught nondirectively despite the teacher holding a view on it, it is harder to think of cases in which a matter is taught directively despite the teacher being agnostic about it. That should not be surprising if the primary reason for discrepancies between the beliefs one holds and the beliefs one is prepared to impart is that the latter must meet a more demanding evidential standard. Still, we should not rule out the possibility of encountering such cases. Imagine a non-religious teacher who accepts a job in a faith-based school on condition that she is prepared to support the school's confessional aims. When religious questions come up in class discussion, a teacher who has agreed to this condition may feel obliged to give public endorsement to answers she does not herself believe to be true. A conscientious teacher is unlikely to be able to endure these circumstances for long; but there is no doubt that teachers sometimes find themselves in situations like this.

So, the choice between teaching a matter directively and teaching it nondirectively is not a choice between didactic and nondidactic teaching methods, and does not turn simply on whether one holds a view on the matter. It is a choice between raising questions with the aim of leading children to particular answers and raising questions without that aim. In the context of moral inquiry, it is a choice between teaching moral standards in a way that favours the conclusion that they are (or are not) justified and teaching them in a way that is neutral on their justificatory status.

This is not, of course, a choice that has to be made wholesale. One might judge that there is ambiguity about the justificatory status of some moral standards and no ambiguity about the justificatory status of others, and adjust the degree of direction one gives in moral inquiry accordingly. Here moral standards are dealt with on a case-by-case basis, each assessed for the robustness of its supporting arguments before a decision is made about how to teach it. But the possibility of choosing wholesale is by no means excluded. A parent or teacher inclined to think that robust justifications are simply unavailable in the moral sphere may opt for a non-directive approach to moral inquiry across the board. She may elect to manage every discussion of moral standards in the way Dawn manages discussion of the morality of voting: by creating opportunities for children to think carefully about purported reasons for subscribing to moral standards without attempting to persuade them that any such reasons are decisive.

Moral inquiry, then, is inquiry into the justificatory status of moral standards. It is cognitive, in that it is concerned with forming, testing and revising beliefs. And it may or may not be directive, depending on whether there is an intention to persuade inquirers that certain moral standards are (or are not) justified.

Education for full moral commitment

A central aim of moral education is to bring it about that children are *fully committed* to certain moral standards, which is to say that they both subscribe to those standards and believe them to be justified. It should now be clear that any serious attempt to realise that aim requires moral educators to engage in both moral formation and directive moral inquiry. Bringing it about that children subscribe to moral standards is a matter of shaping their conative, affective and behavioural dispositions; bringing it about that they believe moral standards to be justified is a matter of persuading them that there is good reason to subscribe. One cannot educate for full moral commitment without doing both of these things.

It should also now be clear that the problem for moral education described in Chapter One, focusing as it does on the impermissibility of teaching standards as justified when there is reasonable disagreement about them, is, more specifically, a problem for directive moral inquiry. Imparting beliefs to children is educationally unobjectionable when the means of persuasion is the force of relevant evidence and argument, when the beliefs in question are warranted and the warrants are presented for inspection. But matters on which reasonable people reasonably disagree are not settled by the available evidence and argument. To impart beliefs on such matters, one must use some other means of persuasion, and the only other means of persuasion are non-rational ones. Insofar as there is reasonable disagreement about the content and justification of morality, it looks as though directive moral inquiry is bound to be indoctrinatory.

Worries about indoctrination are not, properly speaking, pertinent to the enterprise of moral formation. The process of cultivating moral attitudes and dispositions in children cannot itself be indoctrinatory because attitudes and dispositions are not beliefs, and therefore not the sorts of things that can be indoctrinated. It is certainly possible to do children a disservice by rewarding and punishing them for the wrong things, or in the wrong ways, or by modelling the wrong behaviours and reactions; but these are disservices of a different kind from the one we do children by indoctrinating them. It is also possible to engage in moral formation and directive moral inquiry simultaneously, in such a way that certain interventions are intended to be at once attitude-forming and belief-imparting; but here it is precisely the directive moral inquiry component of the activity that runs the risk of being indoctrinatory.

Nor, of course, are worries about indoctrination very relevant to nondirective moral inquiry. Where a parent or teacher deliberately eschews the aim of per-suading children to believe something, and presents the available evidence and argument as neutrally as possible, she is taking all reasonable steps to avoid indoc-trination. Inadvertent indoctrination may still occur: perhaps she feels obliged to give her own view when asked, and perhaps her charismatic hold over her charges is such that some of them adopt the view simply because it is hers. But her non-directive approach minimises the risk of non-rational belief transmission by emphasising the openness of the question under consideration.

So the problem for moral education posed by reasonable disagreement about morality pertains specifically to directive moral inquiry. This suggests a possible response to the problem that may initially seem to have more going for it than the three standard responses considered in Chapter One. Moral educators could simply do without directive moral inquiry. They could sidestep the charge of indoctrina-tion by opting for moral formation alone, or for a combination of moral formation and nondirective moral inquiry. This would be to give up on the aim of bringing it about that children believe moral standards to be justified, but that may be a price worth paying if the aim of bringing about subscription to moral standards can still be realised and educational impropriety is avoided.

Imagine a parent who subscribes to a Christian moral code on theological grounds and wants her children to share her moral standards, but who is also determined to respect her children's autonomy in matters of religion. She knows it is within her power to pass on her religious beliefs by non-rational means, but she wants her children to come to faith by choice, not by manipulation or pressure. Yet she recognises that the acquisition of moral intentions, feelings and habits cannot wait upon the attainment of religious autonomy. Such a parent might well favour a formation-only approach to moral education, or an approach that com-bines moral formation with nondirective moral inquiry. This allows her to mould her children's dispositions in accordance with her Christian moral code without having to persuade them of its theological grounds. She may either ignore the question of justification or raise it in such a way as to keep it open, but she is released from the task of imparting justificatory beliefs.

If doing without directive moral inquiry looks like a more attractive response to the problem of reasonable moral disagreement than the standard responses already discussed (doing without moral education, biting the indoctrination bullet and educating about morality), I think the appearance is deceptive. Giving up on the aim of persuading children that their moral standards are justified is no small sacrifice. Educating merely for moral subscription, and not for full moral commitment, is problematic for at least two reasons.

First, as noted in Chapter Two, those who subscribe to standards without believing them to be justified are deprived of their best weapon against flagging resolve, and the deprivation is most sorely felt when the standards are moral ones. Conflicts between what we desire and what our moral code demands of us are sometimes acute, and such conflicts prompt us to interrogate not only our desires but our code too. What is it, we ask, that gives our moral standards their authority, that makes it rational for us to overrule our desires when they tempt us to do what our standards prohibit? Sometimes we need to remind ourselves of the answer to this question before we can find the strength of will to resist temptation. But if we subscribe to our moral standards in the absence of justificatory beliefs, if we do not know what gives them their authority, we cannot issue such self-reminders.

The inability to bring to mind good reasons for moral subscription not only makes us more vulnerable in moments of temptation, but also tends over time to weaken subscription itself. Other things being equal, the more often it occurs to me that I cannot justify my moral standards, the less steadfast I will become in holding myself and others to them. This is not to deny the indubitable truth that human beings often want, feel and behave in ways that are inconsistent with their own best judgment about what they have reason to want, feel and do; it is just to note that our conative, affective and behavioural dispositions can be quickened or dulled, and one way to dull them is to leave them unsupported by reason.

Second, notwithstanding my insistence on the distinction between moral formation and directive moral inquiry and the possibility of pursuing them independently, in practice the two usually work in tandem and attempting the former in isolation from the latter would present some significant challenges. Children will comply with prescriptions issued by adults, will accept punishments for non-compliance, and will emulate rule-following modelled by those around them; but they will also ask *why* the prescriptions are being issued, the punishments meted out and the rules followed. And they will expect their questions to be satisfactorily answered, if not in the heat of the formative moment, then in the aftermath of the intervention, when the command has been obeyed or the punishment served. Each time their questions are ignored or evaded, they become a little less inclined to comply, accept or emulate on the next occasion. To adopt a systematic policy of ignoring or evading children's justificatory questions is therefore to risk rendering the methods of moral formation ineffective.

I do not suggest that children's 'why' questions are always genuine requests for justification. Sometimes they are best understood as diversionary tactics, or expressions of resistance to adult authority. A child may know quite well what he has done wrong and why he is being punished, yet still try to put off the inevitable by feigning incomprehension. On other occasions, 'why' questions are asked because children want to understand how moral standards bear on an action they have been instructed to take, or punished for not taking. 'Why have I got to put this back?' may be quite adequately answered by 'Because it belongs to your sister and you cannot take things that belong to other people without asking'. But 'why' questions cannot always be construed in these ways: sometimes children really are asking about the justification of the moral standards to which they are being held. And the eschewal of directive moral inquiry leaves parents and teachers unable to supply them with answers.

For these two reasons, moral educators should be extremely reluctant to abandon the central aim of cultivating full moral commitment, of bringing it about that children subscribe to moral standards *and* believe them to be justified. A formation-only approach to moral education, or an approach that combines moral formation with nondirective moral inquiry, is inadequate, in part because the tools of moral formation are blunted if children's justificatory questions go unanswered, and in part because it is harder for moral agents to hold themselves to moral standards if they cannot see the reasons for them. The pressing question, then, is not whether we can do without directive moral inquiry, but rather, given the need to persuade children that certain moral standards are justified, whether this can be achieved without recourse to indoctrination.

4

CONSENSUS ON CONTENT

Indoctrination looks hard to avoid in moral education because of reasonable disagreement about the content and justification of morality. People reasonably disagree about which moral standards they should subscribe to and why they should subscribe to them. As noted in Chapter One, however, reasonable disagreement on the content of morality is not absolute. While people are divided on the morality of voting, meat-eating and smacking, they are not divided – or are at any rate much less divided – on the morality of lying, cheating and stealing. They may justify their moral codes in quite different ways, but there is a significant overlap between the codes themselves.

The phenomenon of consensus on the content of morality, even in the absence of consensus on its justification, has seemed to some to offer hope of a way out of the indoctrination bind. Perhaps consensus on content opens the door to a kind of second-order justification of morality. If one knows that there are standards to which more or less everyone subscribes, or standards on which most first-order justifications converge, perhaps one has good reason to subscribe to those standards, even if one has yet to pin one's colours to any first-order justificatory mast. If so, moral educators may be able to offer children this second-order justification for moral subscription and thus avoid any impropriety in the conduct of directive moral inquiry. That is the possibility I shall consider in this chapter.

Commonly agreed standards

The last serious attempt by a UK government to get to grips with moral education in schools was made 20 years ago, in 1996, when the Schools Curriculum and Assessment Authority (SCAA) set up the National Forum for Values in Education and the Community. The Forum's remit was to:

1. discover whether there are any values upon which there is common agreement within society;
2. decide how schools might be supported in the important task of contributing to pupils' spiritual, moral, social and cultural development.

(SCAA, 1997, p.10)

The Forum had 150 members 'drawn from across society' and went about its work through a series of group discussion meetings, 'with conclusions from each meeting being passed to the other groups before the next meeting' (Talbot and Tate, 1997, p.2). Its deliberations yielded a Statement of Values and an accompanying Preamble (SCAA, 1997, pp.10–14), versions of which were for many years appended to the National Curriculum for England.

I think the Forum's work can fairly be construed as an attempt to solve the problem with which we are presently concerned: the threat to moral education posed by reasonable moral disagreement. But let me acknowledge immediately that it was concerned with some other things too, and, indeed, that there is a certain lack of clarity about the nature and scope of its concerns. These complicating factors make my construal of the Forum's work a little controversial, so it is worth taking a few moments to defend it.

First, the Forum set out in search of commonly agreed *values*, and it is plain that values come in more shapes and sizes than moral standards. It is, to be sure, not easy to say just what a value is – and the vagueness of the term may well have been a factor in the SCAA's decision to use it. But that the Forum's remit was to explore a somewhat wider range of values than moral ones is indicated by the aim of supporting schools in their contribution to pupils' spiritual, social and cultural development as well as their moral development. Nevertheless, there is abundant evidence that the primary focus of the Forum's efforts was the articulation of a shared moral code. For one thing, the majority of the 33 'shoulds' in the final Statement of Values are much more plausibly classified as moral than as spiritual, social or cultural. For another, the SCAA Discussion Paper that recommended the establishment of the Forum is heavily preoccupied with the need for moral education in schools. Among the key points summarised at the start of the document are that 'Many pressures work against clear moral principles and behaviour' and that 'For some children, school is the only place where they will encounter moral teaching' (SCAA, 1996, p.5). Graham Haydon, an erstwhile member of the Forum, argues that the social concerns in response to which the Forum was created made it inevitable that the common values identified would be moral ones:

What was aimed at when the Forum was set up (given the background from which that move had come) was something which could influence how people across society would behave. If we are trying to draw up an itemised statement of what people should do, where the items in the statement are to apply to everyone, and there is to be wide agreement on the items across society, then moral values are what we are going to get, because this (on one plausible understanding of morality) is the sort of thing moral values are.

(Haydon, 1999, p.26)

Second, the Forum's attention to moral education was motivated by a broader set of worries than the problem of reasonable moral disagreement. The most immediate and pressing of these were worries about moral degeneration and social breakdown. In the SCAA Discussion Paper there is much hand-wringing about our 'living in a time of moral crisis', society being 'rife with drug abuse, crime and violence', and the young being 'out of control' (SCAA, 1996, p.8). Also to the fore were anxieties about the effect on children of advertising, consumerism and unsalubrious aspects of popular culture. But the fact that members of the Forum entertained worries of this kind does not count against the claim that they were also exercised by the challenge of reasonable moral disagreement. If the former convinced them that more rigorous moral education in schools was necessary, the latter represented the chief obstacle to be overcome. The cautionary thought that 'it is difficult to promote common values in a heterogeneous society' is recorded at the outset in the SCAA Discussion Paper (ibid., p.19). And the Forum's sensitivity to the problem is clearly evident in the Preamble, where agreement on values is sharply distinguished from agreement on the sources of value:

> Agreement on the values outlined below is compatible with disagreement on their sources. Many believe that God is the ultimate source of value, and that we are accountable to God for our actions; others that values have their source only in human nature, and that we are accountable only to our consciences. The statement of values is consistent with these and other views on the sources of value.
>
> *(SCAA, 1997, p.11)*

Third, there is some ambiguity about the extent to which the Forum intended the values in the Statement to be actively promoted in schools. Haydon has suggested that the Statement might best be seen as a springboard for classroom discussion rather than an authoritative moral code:

> So what is the use of the resulting statement? Teachers from other countries often tell me about their statements of values that the schools are expected to inculcate. That is not the English way … The educational value of the statement could be to see it as a set of reference points, in which the fact that there was widespread agreement on the values included is not the end of the matter, but a starting point for discussion.
>
> *(Haydon, 2007, p.10)*

But if Haydon's remark about 'the English way' is intended to suggest that the work of the Forum was never motivated by a concern with moral formation and direction, we should treat it with caution. One of the principal justifications for establishing the Forum, as set out in the SCAA Discussion Paper, was that 'national assent to core values would give schools authority and confidence in promoting them' (SCAA, 1996, p.19). Marianne Talbot and Nick Tate, respectively Chair of the Forum and Chief Executive of the SCAA, were in no doubt that, to the question '*whose* values are we supposed to instill?', there is 'a simple and empirically justifiable answer: namely, *our* values' (Talbot and Tate, 1997, p.1). And the claim in the Preamble that the Statement 'neither implies nor entails that these are the *only* values that should be taught in schools' (SCAA, 1997, p.11) makes clear that these values *at least* should be taught, as does the promise of support and encouragement from society if schools and teachers 'base their teaching and the school ethos on these values' (ibid.).

Fourth, and finally, objections might be raised to the idea that the Forum was troubled by the problem of indoctrination, by educational scruples about non-rational belief transmission. Here, I concede, supporting evidence is thin on the ground. It may well be that some, perhaps many, members of the Forum were willing to sanction the use of non-rational methods to persuade children that subscription to widely shared moral values is justified. But that there was at least some concern with the provision of reasons is indicated by the stipulation in the SCAA Discussion Paper that morally developed young people should be 'knowledgeable about standards of right and wrong' and 'skilled in moral reasoning' (SCAA, 1996, p.9). Good behaviour, it is argued, is not itself indicative of morality, because 'Good behaviour can be instilled by rigorous training or fear of punishment, rather than by an understanding of why such behaviour is desirable, right or necessary' (ibid.). Insofar as the Forum worked on the assumption that morality involves *understanding why* some actions are required or prohibited, there cannot have been complete disregard for the place of reason in moral education.

I shall take it, then, that the members of the Forum were at least partly concerned with the threat to moral education that interests us here. What was the solution they proposed?

To the question of whether there is agreement on values across society, the Forum responded with a resounding yes. 'Almost as soon as they considered the question', report Talbot and Tate, 'they came up with a number of values to which, they believed, everyone would subscribe' (Talbot and Tate, 1997, p.2). In a subsequent MORI poll of 1500 adults, some 95 per cent agreed with the values in the Forum's Statement. This, Talbot and Tate declare, 'conclusively established' that 'the values identified by the Forum are values upon which everyone of goodwill will agree' (ibid., p.3).

There are some obvious worries here: about what is involved in conclusively establishing claims of this kind, about the size and representativeness of both the Forum and the survey sample, about the one in 20 people who disagreed with the Statement of Values, and about the slippage from 'everyone' to 'everyone of goodwill'. I shall, however, set these worries aside and move directly to the second step of the Forum's solution: the inference from the claim that there are values shared by everyone of goodwill to the claim that those values can properly be promoted in schools.

Recall the crucial distinction in the Preamble between agreement on values and agreement on the sources of value. The Forum explicitly endorses the view that the values shared across society are rooted for some in beliefs about God and for others in beliefs about human nature. Different members of society explain and justify the values they share in different ways. So when the Forum infers from the fact of agreement on these values the recommendation that they be promoted in schools, how is it envisaged that children will be persuaded of their authority? Are teachers just to insist bullishly on their authority until children lose the will to resist? Are they to plump arbitrarily for one of the contested justifications and pretend that it is rationally decisive? Or is the thought that consensus on content can ground a justificatory argument of an entirely different order?

At least some influential members of the Forum seem to have been tempted by this last thought. In discussing the significance of the Forum's findings, Talbot and Tate do not argue that there is a fortuitous overlap between *agreed* and *justified* moral values; rather they argue that agreement on moral values itself carries justificatory weight. They stop short of proposing that their agreement-based justification is the one that should be offered to children in schools, but this is a natural implication of their view, at least insofar as they are committed to a directive and rational form of moral education.

So how does their argument work? According to Talbot and Tate, a foundation of moral agreement is a necessary condition of rational moral discourse. Without it, they contend, disagreements 'become meaningless', 'argument would be pointless' and 'truth would be forever beyond our grasp' (ibid., p.6). They write:

> Argument – the means by which human beings search for truth – is wholly dependent upon the existence of some basic agreement. We can potentially convince each other of our conclusions only if we can rely upon agreement on the premises and upon the steps of the argument itself.
>
> *(ibid.)*

Unless we can argue rationally about moral questions, we cannot hope to establish anything in the moral sphere, so moral agreement is needed to 'lay the foundations for the acquisition of moral knowledge' (ibid. p.8).

What Talbot and Tate seem to have in mind here is some version of the familiar Wittgensteinian thesis that 'Understanding in language requires not only agreement in definitions, but also (queer as this may sound) agreement in judgments' (Wittgenstein, 1953, Section 242). There must be agreement, that is to say, not only on how the words of a language are definitionally related to one another, but also on how they are used to refer to and describe the world. If we are using the same words but cannot agree on the truth of any proposition in which they are deployed, we do not really understand each other.

Talbot and Tate's second-order justification for subscription to agreed moral values is therefore as follows:

1. General agreement on a set of moral values is a condition of the possibility of rational moral discourse.
2. Rational moral discourse is desirable.
3. Therefore we ought to subscribe to the set of moral values on which there is general agreement.

This is fairly unpersuasive, and for several reasons. First, someone wondering why they should subscribe to moral standards at all is unlikely to be impressed by the claim that doing so is a precondition of rational moral discourse. If, for example, one suspects that morality is a system of arbitrary constraints on conduct imposed by the powerful on the powerless to keep them in their place, one will not be too worried by the thought that refusal to fall in line chips away at the consensus on which the edifice of moral knowledge is built. Similarly, if one finds presumptuous the very idea of holding others to the standards one has chosen to live by, one will have little investment in the resolvability of disagreements about which standards merit universally-enlisting subscription.

Second, while it may be true that understanding a language requires agreement in judgments as well as definitions, it is implausible to suppose that moral discourse constitutes a language in the relevant sense. We might, perhaps, think of normative discourse in general as a Wittgensteinian 'language game', understanding of which involves agreement on at least some reasons for subscribing to at least some standards. But morality is just one region of normative discourse, perfectly intelligible to players of the normative language game prior to any agreement on specifically moral standards. In principle, at least, there need be no overlap at all between your moral standards and mine for us to engage in rational discussion about whether a specified standard is justified.

Talbot and Tate use the debate on abortion to illustrate the alleged dependence of rational moral discourse on agreed moral values:

> If we didn't agree on the fact that both human life and individual choice should be respected, then the abortion debate would be impossible. We disagree so violently because each side believes that the other's acceptance of the premise – that human life, or human choice, ought to be respected – should entail the other's acceptance of the conclusion. If we couldn't agree on the premises, there would be no argument.
>
> *(Talbot and Tate, 1997, p.7)*

Here the abortion debate is couched as a disagreement about whether a prohibition on abortion is or is not entailed by moral standards the debaters share. This is certainly an important kind of moral disagreement, and one to which there is at least hope of rational resolution. But there are plenty of moral disagreements that do not take this form and do not thereby cease to be rational. The debate about the morality of voting, for example, is rarely taken to turn on what is or is not entailed by accepted moral standards. Parties to the debate typically focus on the reasons we might have for wanting everyone to vote and whether those reasons are strong enough to justify universally-enlisting and penalty-endorsing subscription to a standard. They argue from first principles, so to speak, not from shared moral premises. Debates about abortion can be like this too: sometimes debaters are not disagreeing about what is entailed by the acknowledged moral right of women to control their own bodies, but rather about whether such a moral right should be recognised.

So it is hard to see why we should accept the claim that rational moral debate would be impossible without agreed moral values. Moral discourse is not a closed linguistic loop, accessible only to those who assent to its axioms, but part of the larger universe of normative discourse. The moral sceptic who holds that no moral standards are justified may be mistaken, but she is not someone to whom moral discourse is unintelligible, with whom moral argument would be pointless, or whose mind on moral matters cannot be changed by the presentation of good reasons.

Third, even if it were to be conceded that agreement on a set of moral values is a condition of the possibility of rational moral discourse, there remains a crucial distinction between the values on which agreement is necessary and the values on which there happens to be agreement in a particular society at a particular time. Why should it be assumed that the moral values shared by people of goodwill in England in the mid-1990s are co-extensive with the moral values presupposed by rational moral discourse? At least some of the values in the Statement (the require-ment to 'support the institution of marriage', for example) look less like axioms of moral discourse than social preferences illegitimately elevated to the status of moral principles. A second-order justification of the kind Talbot and Tate favour shows at best that we must take *some* moral standards on faith in order to participate in moral argument and discussion; it emphatically does not show that we must take on faith the full set of moral standards to which members of our society currently subscribe.

For these reasons, the solution to the educational problem of reasonable moral disagreement proposed by the National Forum for Values in Education and the Community must be rejected.

Standards supported by an overlapping consensus

Perhaps the most sustained philosophical attempt to make normative consensus do serious justificatory work is John Rawls' defence of his political conception of justice with reference to the idea of an 'overlapping consensus' of reasonable comprehensive doctrines. We noted in Chapter One that the question Rawls asks is: 'how is it possible for there to exist over time a just and stable society of free and equal citizens who remain profoundly divided by reasonable religious, philosophical and moral doctrines?' (Rawls, 2005, p.4). The answer he offers is that a society of this kind must be regulated by a political conception of justice that can gain the support of 'a reasonable and enduring overlapping consensus' (ibid., p.40). We should endorse justice as fairness (the political conception Rawls favours) at least partly because it is capable of gaining such support.

A political conception of justice is not, of course, a moral code in the sense that presently interests us. The thought I would like to pursue, though, is that Rawls' proposed justificatory strategy might be transposed from the political domain to the moral one. If a capacity to gain the support of a reasonable overlapping consensus can serve to justify a political conception of justice, might it not serve to justify a moral code too? My aim, in other words, is not to assess the adequacy of Rawls' answer to the question he asks, but to assess the adequacy of a Rawlsian-style answer to the question before us now. I do not suggest that this Rawlsian-style answer is one to which Rawls himself would have been sympathetic.

Let us begin by looking more closely at Rawls' argument for justice as fairness. It is, he says, an argument that involves 'three different kinds of justification', which he labels 'pro tanto justification', 'full justification' and 'public justification' (ibid., pp.385–386). The first of these, pro tanto justification, consists in collecting up and coherently organising people's settled political convictions. Rawls describes the process like this:

> We collect such settled convictions as the belief in religious toleration and the rejection of slavery and try to organise the basic ideas and principles implicit in these convictions into a coherent political conception of justice. These convictions are provisional fixed points that it seems any reasonable conception must account for. We start, then, by looking to the public culture itself as the shared fund of implicitly recognised basic ideas and principles. We hope to formulate these ideas and principles clearly enough to be combined into a political conception of justice congenial to our most firmly held convictions.
>
> *(ibid., p.8)*

This process of collecting, distilling, organising and formulating, of moving back and forth between firm convictions, implicit ideas and general conceptions, is what Rawls calls the method of reflective equilibrium. If, by using this method, we can order and balance our political values in such a way as to answer 'all or nearly all questions concerning constitutional essentials and basic justice' (ibid., p.386), our political conception is pro tanto justified.

The next question we must each ask ourselves is whether we can square our pro tanto justified political conception with the comprehensive doctrine to which we adhere. By a comprehensive doctrine Rawls means a general normative scheme that 'includes conceptions of what is of value in human life, and ideals of personal character, as well as ideals of friendship and of familial and associational relationships, and much else that is to inform our conduct, and in the limit to our life as a whole' (ibid., p.13). It is a working assumption for Rawls that everyone affirms some such normative scheme, even if its elements are only loosely articulated. Once we have achieved internal coherence among our settled political convictions, then, we must seek external coherence between our political convictions and our other values and ideals. When we achieve this, our political conception is said to enjoy full justification.

Rawls is at pains to emphasise that, in this second justificatory stage, we are not further adjusting our conception of justice to make it compatible with our comprehensive doctrines, but rather adjusting our comprehensive doctrines to make them compatible with our conception of justice. We should have great confidence in our pro tanto justified political conception and be ready to revise or reorder our non-political values to accommodate it. 'A reasonable and effective political conception', says Rawls, 'may bend comprehensive doctrines toward itself, shaping them if need be from unreasonable to reasonable' (ibid., p.246). The process of achieving full justification is therefore one of embedding or inserting a political conception into a comprehensive doctrine, adapting the hole to the peg if the initial fit is poor.

The citizen who has forged a coherent conception of justice from her settled political convictions, and squared it with her non-political values and ideals, has done all she can to justify it. But she is not yet entitled to regard it as justified. A conception of justice lays down principles for regulating the exercise of political power, and 'political power is always coercive power' (ibid., p.68). In endorsing such a conception a citizen is not merely agreeing to be coerced; she is agreeing to the coercion of others. So it is not enough for her to have succeeded in embedding the conception in her own comprehensive doctrine. She must additionally know that her fellow citizens have succeeded in embedding it in theirs. This is what Rawls means by public justification: 'Public justification happens when all the reasonable members of political society carry out a justification of the shared political conception by embedding it in their several reasonable comprehensive views' (ibid., p.387).

From the point of view of the individual citizen whose conception of justice has passed the tests of pro tanto and full justification, this final justificatory stage is a matter of waiting and hoping. She cannot do other people's embedding for them. And if some of her fellow citizens find that they cannot square a pro tanto justified political conception with their non-political values – if, that is, the conception fails the test of public justification – she must admit that exercises of coercive power on the basis of that conception are illegitimate.

When all citizens succeed in embedding a pro tanto justified political conception in their respective comprehensive doctrines, we may say that the conception has gained the support of a reasonable overlapping consensus. Rawls distinguishes his notion of a reasonable overlapping consensus from the idea of consensus that 'comes from everyday politics' (ibid., p.389), whereby political use is made of the fact that people happen to agree on certain things. The claim is not that people happen to agree on a conception of justice. A reasonable overlapping consensus is rather an ambitious political goal, to be achieved by working out a coherent conception of justice and asking all citizens to embed it in their comprehensive doctrines. It is Rawls' hope that justice as fairness can gain the support of an overlapping consensus of this kind.

So goes Rawls' three-stage justification for his favoured political conception. Now let me sketch a structurally similar justification for a moral code of conduct. Suppose, first, that we find in the public culture a loose assortment of settled moral convictions and implicit moral ideas and principles, and that, through a process of collecting, distilling and organising, we construct from these a coherent moral code. We use the method of reflective equilibrium to balance our moral values in such a way as to answer all or nearly all questions about required and prohibited forms of conduct.

Suppose, second, that each of us is asked to embed the resulting moral code in our wider normative schemes. In addition to our moral standards – those to which our subscription is univerally-enlisting and penalty-endorsing – we each subscribe to numerous non-moral standards, values and ideals that guide our conduct in a variety of different contexts. So it makes good sense to consider how well our moral code coheres with our other normative commitments.

And suppose, finally, that, before fully committing ourselves, each of us is asked to wait and see whether everyone else can embed the moral code in their wider normative schemes too. Because of its universally-enlisting and penalty-endorsing character, morality is an inherently coercive enterprise, so we should check that the moral code we adopt can also be adopted by all those whose conduct will be regulated by it. We should look, that is to say, for the support of an overlapping consensus.

Here, then, is a Rawlsian-style justification for subscription to a moral code. Recall that our question is whether there is a second-order, consensus-based justification for moral subscription that might be offered to children in lieu of a compelling first-order justification. Does this Rawlsian-style argument fit the bill?

We may observe immediately that it does not, for one reason in particular: the notion of consensus does not do nearly enough heavy lifting in the argument for it to qualify as consensus-based. Consensus only enters the justificatory picture at stage three, when the proposed moral code has already passed the tests of pro tanto and full justification and the individual inquirer is poised to endorse it. The final test of public justification is needed because it matters that others can see the reasons for the standards we hold them to: if consensus really cannot be reached, we may all have to go back to the drawing board. But the achievement of consensus on a moral code adds nothing to the individual inquirer's positive reasons for assenting to it. It simply removes one kind of reason for withholding assent.

Integral as it is to the structure of Rawls' argument, there is no suggestion that the achievement of overlapping consensus serves as a substitute for first-order justification. In the case for justice as fairness, by far the greatest justificatory burden is borne by the pro tanto argument: it is the capacity of a political conception to knit together our firm political convictions and fundamental political ideas that gives us grounds to adopt it. So strong are the grounds it gives us that we are prepared to amend our comprehensive doctrines to accommodate it, and hopeful that others will be prepared to amend theirs. To be sure, justice as fairness will be defeated if it cannot gain the support of a reasonable overlapping consensus; but whether or not it clears this final hurdle is a separate matter from whether or not we have good reason to back it.

There may well be a justified moral code that we can all successfully embed in our wider normative schemes; but it is not the universal embeddability of the code that justifies it. The demand for justification precedes the hope for consensus: we begin by asking whether a moral code deserves our allegiance and only when we have concluded that it does do we wonder if some will find the price of allegiance too high to pay. To tell children that a moral code has gained the support of an overlapping consensus is not, therefore, to give them a reason to endorse it. At most it is to give them one less impediment to endorsement to worry about.

This consideration suffices to show that a Rawlsian-style justification for morality does not qualify as a consensus-based argument of the kind we are looking for. It does not give us a way of sidestepping the first-order justificatory question in directive moral education. Still, it is worth asking whether it might help us with our problem in a different way. If it does not pass muster as a second-order justification of morality, does it constitute a more robust and educationally serviceable first-order justification than the available alternatives?

If the real justificatory work in the Rawlsian schema is done at the pro tanto stage, by the method of reflective equilibrium, the claim would have to be that a moral code is justified when it coherently knits together a person's settled moral convictions and the moral ideas implicit in them. The obvious problem with this claim is that it seems to defer the justificatory question rather than answer it. Sure, one wants to say, if you use only justified moral convictions, you should be able to build a justified moral code; but how will you establish that your moral convictions are justified in the first place? The method of reflective equilibrium may well enable us to transfer justification from the parts to the whole, but it cannot enable us to conjure justification out of nothing. If our moral convictions happen to be wrong, and it is surely not contentious to suggest that people's moral convictions sometimes *are* wrong, we shall not find our way to a justified moral code by moving back and forth between them.

Aside from this basic worry about what the method of reflective equilibrium can achieve, there is a particular difficulty about using it in the context of moral education. The method is only available to people already in possession of settled moral convictions. If I am confident in at least some of my moral judgments, I can start to ask questions about the principles they imply and use my judgments and principles to construct a moral code. But children are precisely those whose moral convictions are least likely to be settled, who may not yet be confident about any of their moral judgments. The questions they have are not, or not only, about whether and how their moral intuitions can be coherently fitted together, but rather, or also, about whether and why their moral intuitions are to be trusted. Reflective equilibrium starts too high up, as it were; it can perhaps help the mature moral agent troubled by inconsistencies in her moral thinking, but it has little to offer to the moral neophyte wondering if she needs moral standards at all.

As for the test of full justification, being fitted into a wider normative scheme is a less impressive achievement for a moral code than for a political conception of justice. It is precisely because political justice is only one area of moral concern, and because for most of us the other areas are just as important, that Rawls thinks we must find a way to square justice as fairness with our comprehensive doctrines. We shall run into difficulty if our political morality is at odds with our non-political morality. But in the present case full justification is only a matter of fitting a moral code into a wider set of non-moral values. Since we normally regard moral considerations as significantly weightier than non-moral considerations, there is little need for a deliberative process of adjusting and embedding here: the fit is achieved simply by giving priority to moral standards. In this sense, any moral code is easily squared with any wider normative scheme, so passing the full justification test is a fairly meagre accomplishment.

And again, there are obvious difficulties about using this test with children whose moral and non-moral values are still under construction or in a state of flux. The test assumes the existence of both a worked-out moral code and a wider normative framework, about whose compatibility sensible questions can be asked. But this assumption cannot reasonably be made in the context of the moral education of children.

I conclude that the Rawlsian model of justification does not help us with our problem (though let me emphasise again that our problem is not the one Rawls sets out to solve). It does not furnish us with a second-order, consensus-based justification for morality that would allow us to shelve first-order justificatory debate for the purposes of directive moral education. And the first-order justification with which it does furnish us is not nearly compelling enough to escape the reasonable disagreement that besets other first order justifications.

Standards on which moral theories converge

In their influential book *Principles of Biomedical Ethics* (Beauchamp and Childress, 1994), Tom Beauchamp and James Childress argue that different justificatory theories converge on basically the same moral code. They write:

> Many different theories lead to similar action-guides and to similar estimates of the role of character in ethics. It is possible from several of these standpoints to defend roughly the same principles, obligations, rights, responsibilities and virtues … It is a mistake to suppose that a series of continental divides separates moral theorists into distinct and hostile groups who reach different practical conclusions and fail to converge on principles.
>
> *(ibid., pp.110–111)*

The significance of this convergence, for Beauchamp and Childress, is that fundamental disagreement at the level of moral justification need not infect the process of collective moral deliberation. Because different justificatory theories yield more or less the same moral standards, questions about how to apply those standards to particular cases, or to particular types of case, can be tackled collectively by groups of people with quite different moral theoretical commitments. The standards on which Beauchamp and Childress think moral theories converge are the four general principles of respect for autonomy, nonmaleficence, beneficence and justice.

The question I should like to consider here is whether, in addition to its significance for collective moral deliberation, moral theoretical convergence could also serve as the basis of a second-order justification. Suppose it were to be claimed that *all* available justificatory theories (not just some or many of them) converge on the same moral code. The theories conflict with each other, so cannot all be right, and we are not in a position to say which of them is the right one; but since they all purport to justify the same set of standards, perhaps we *are* in a position to say that the standards in question are justified. We might think of the various theories as being differentiated by their starting points, and of the disagreement over starting points as being resistant to settlement; but if the argumentative path from each starting point leads to the same destination, can we not infer that the conclusion must be sound? If all roads lead to Rome, Rome is presumably where we are bound to end up.

Note that this convergence-based justification is not technically an argument from consensus. There can be consensus on a moral code without it being the case that all moral theories converge on it, and moral theories can converge on a code without it being the case all or most people subscribe to it. But it does qualify as a second-order argument in the sense that it sidesteps the question of which first-order justification is successful. And, of course, if there is both a convergence of moral theories and a consensus on moral content, the two facts are surely connected.

An all-roads-lead-to-Rome justification of morality would certainly help with the problem of avoiding indoctrination in directive moral education. Teachers would not need to persuade children to sign up to a controversial first-order justification; they would need only persuade them that all first-order justificatory theories yield the same set of moral standards, and that this is reason enough to endorse those standards. Children can then decide for themselves whether to take sides in moral theoretical debate or to reserve judgment until such time as a good reason to favour one moral theory over others comes to light.

Unfortunately, however, the objections to a justification along these lines are legion. First, while it is true that some rival justificatory theories yield some of the same moral standards, the extent of the overlap is easily exaggerated. There are striking differences between the moral codes typically defended by, for example, utilitarians, Kantians and divine command theorists. If the sets of moral standards generated by just these three theories were represented on a Venn diagram, each of the seven regions would likely be populated: there would be standards unique to each set, standards shared by two sets but not the third, and standards shared by all three. From the fact that there would be something in the central intersection, it does not follow that the three theories are well described as convergent. Moreover, the moral code that consists only of the standards in this intersection is not the moral code for which utilitarians, Kantians or divine command theorists argue.

Second, it is manifestly false that *all* theoretical attempts on the problem of moral justification result in endorsement of a core set of moral standards. Some such attempts result in moral scepticism, the view that we have insufficient reason to endorse any moral standard. The fact that some moral theoretical journeys terminate in moral scepticism is enough to show that not all roads lead to Rome. But once it is admitted that some roads lead elsewhere, the proposed second-order justification collapses entirely: if destinations vary, it matters a great deal which first-order argumentative path one chooses to follow.

Third, even if it were true that all of the available justificatory theories converged on the same moral code, it would not follow that the code were justified. Conflicting and controversial arguments do not cease to be conflicting and controversial simply because they all point to the same conclusion. Insofar as the arguments conflict, one cannot think of them as making a cumulative case, so one's warrant for accepting the conclusion is only as strong as the strongest argument. And insofar as the arguments are controversial, the strongest of them may not be strong enough. Convergence alone cannot mend the deficiencies in first-order justifications for morality that prompted the quest for a second-order justification in the first place.

An analogy may help here. A century ago there was widespread agreement among speakers of the English language on the authority of the standard 'don't split infinitives'. But different grammarians deployed different arguments to justify the rule. One argument was descriptivist: competent English speakers do not, in fact, split infinitives, so anyone wishing to speak English competently ought likewise to refrain from doing so. Another argument was that the full infinitive is a single linguistic unit, so its two parts must not be divided. Still another was that the grammatical template for the English language is set by Latin, and in Latin infinitives cannot be split.

Now imagine an Edwardian teacher, charged with inculcating in her pupils a deep-seated aversion to infinitive-splitting, but wanting to furnish them with a sound justification for the prohibition. Perhaps she might be tempted by an all-roads-lead-to-Rome argument: the justifications offered by grammarians are multiple and contested, but they all support the conclusion that infinitives should not be split; so one may safely infer that splitting infinitives is wrong.

Such an argument would have been bogus, for obvious reasons. For one thing, rational objections to the prohibition were by no means unknown in the early 1900s. That clarity and economy of expression sometimes require separating the parts of a full infinitive was a perfectly familiar point, made, for example, by George Bernard Shaw in a letter to *The Times* in 1907:

> There is a busybody on your staff who devotes a lot of time to chasing split infinitives. Every good literary craftsman splits his infinitives when the sense demands it. I call for the immediate dismissal of this pedant. It is of no

consequence whether he decides to go quickly, or quickly to go, or to quickly go. The important thing is that he should go at once.

(Shaw, cited in Gowers, 2015, p.234)

For another thing, none of the grammarians' arguments in support of the prohibition is strong: the descriptivist claim about the behaviour of competent English speakers is (and was) false; the argument that infinitives cannot be split because linguistic units cannot be divided is question-begging; and in Latin infinitives never have two parts, so the question of splitting does not arise. It is, of course, for just these reasons that few grammarians today are prepared to defend the rule.

Just as our Edwardian teacher should resist the temptation of an all-roads-lead-to-Rome argument in the teaching of split infinitives, so moral educators should resist the temptation of such an argument in the teaching of morals. To be sure, when distinct lines of argument converge, or even partially converge, on a widely-accepted conclusion, the phenomenon stands in need of explanation. But by no means all of the possible explanations support the idea that the conclusion is justified. The explanation might be that large numbers of people have been socialised to accept some more or less arbitrary norm and have then cast around for plausible-looking post hoc justifications, resulting in a motley collection of specious arguments converging on a predetermined conclusion. That would seem to be the best explanation for the general consensus and argumentative convergence on the infinitive-splitting prohibition a hundred years ago. Perhaps it is also the best explanation for whatever consensus and argumentative convergence there might be on the content of morality today.

5

JUSTIFIED MORAL STANDARDS

The problem for moral education posed by reasonable disagreement about morality cannot be solved by appeal to consensus on content, or to the idea that rival justificatory theories converge. Non-indoctrinatory directive moral inquiry is only possible if there is a robust first-order justification for subscription to moral standards that children can be helped to grasp. But is it not an implication of reasonable disagreement about morality that no such justification is available?

Not quite. Let us remind ourselves of the ways in which people reasonably disagree about the content and justification of morality. First, there are many standards such that it is an open question whether or not moral subscription to them is justified. Some reasonable people feel justified in subscribing morally, others in subscribing only non-morally, and still others do not feel justified in subscribing at all. Second, there are many arguments for moral subscription such that it is an open question whether or not they are sound. The arguments are persuasive to some reasonable people but not to others. Rational dispute about the justificatory status of these standards and the soundness of these arguments looks set to be a salient feature of our moral landscape for the foreseeable future.

But it would be premature to infer from this state of affairs that no moral standards are robustly justified. From the fact that some moral standards have an uncertain justificatory status, it does not follow that all do; and the fact that some arguments for moral subscription are questionable does not entail that all are. Perhaps, somewhere in the melee of rationally disputed moral standards and arguments, there are at least some standards whose justificatory status is beyond reasonable doubt, because there is an argument for subscribing to them that has decisive rational force.

I shall argue in this chapter that this is just how things are. The argument rests on two claims. The first is that all human beings, or at least all human beings living alongside others in social groups, are unavoidably confronted with a serious practical problem. Following David Copp, I shall call this the *problem of sociality* (Copp,

2009, p.22). The second is that human beings can effectively ameliorate this problem by means of universally-enlisting and penalty-endorsing subscription to some basic standards of conduct. These two claims together amount to a justification for subscribing to a core moral code that counts decisively in favour of doing so – and which children can therefore be persuaded to accept in the context of directive moral inquiry without recourse to indoctrination.

The problem of sociality

The problem of sociality arises because of three contingent but permanent features of the human condition. These features, sometimes described as the 'circumstances of justice', are (i) rough equality, (ii) limited sympathy and (iii) moderate scarcity of resources. Discussions of these features or circumstances are to be found in the writings of many philosophers, including Thomas Hobbes (1929 [1651]), David Hume (1896 [1739]), H.L.A. Hart (1994 [1961]), G.J. Warnock (1971), John Rawls (1971) and J.L. Mackie (1977). I will say a little about each feature in turn, before explaining the problem to which they collectively give rise.

Hobbes begins his account of 'the natural condition of mankind', in Chapter 13 of *Leviathan*, with the following observation:

> Nature hath made men so equall, in the faculties of body, and mind; as that though there bee found one man sometimes manifestly stronger in body, or of quicker mind then another; yet when all is reckoned together, the difference between man, and man, is not so considerable, as that one man can thereupon claim to himselfe any benefit, to which another may not pretend, as well as he. For as to the strength of body, the weakest has strength enough to kill the strongest, either by secret machination, or by confederacy with others, that are in the same danger with himselfe.
>
> *(Hobbes, 1929 [1651], p.94)*

While human beings differ quite widely in their physical and mental capacities, the variation is within a restricted range. We are *roughly* equal to one another in the sense that we need and want the same sorts of things and are similarly, though not identically, equipped to obtain those things. We have similar appetites and desires; we are capable of acquiring a similar repertoire of manual, linguistic and cognitive skills; and we are susceptible to similar kinds of disease, injury and loss. We are also similarly vulnerable to harm at one another's hands.

This last similarity is especially important. The differences between us are never so great as to make the strongest and fastest immune to attack by the weakest and slowest. Rough equality means that no one can safely ignore the aggression or discontent of others, nor hope to keep it indefinitely at bay by a show of superior strength. As Hart puts it, 'no individual is so much more powerful than others, that he is able, without co-operation, to dominate or subdue them for more than a short period' (Hart, 1994 [1961], p.195). Human history is, of course, littered with attempts by individuals and groups to manage the aggression of other individuals and groups by means of domination and subjugation; but the implication of rough equality (and the lesson of history) is that such attempts are bound to end in failure because the strength of the subjugators does not sufficiently exceed that of the subjugated.

These facts about human beings are contingent ones. It might have been the case that people differed much more radically than they do, in ways that allowed the strong to pay no heed to the weak, or to subdue them effectively and permanently. Or it might have been the case that people, though similar in strength, were not vulnerable to one another: Hart notes that 'there are species of animals whose physical structure (including exoskeletons or a carapace) renders them virtually immune from attack by other members of their species' (ibid., p.194). So there is no necessity about our being roughly equal and vulnerable to one another; but nor is there anything optional or temporary about it. It is just what human beings are like.

The second feature of the human condition that interests us is limited sympathy. Before saying what limited sympathy is, let me say something about what it is not. To say that there are limits on the human capacity for sympathy is emphatically *not* to say that human beings are fundamentally selfish or egoistic. It is not to suggest that people act only in their own interests, or that they are generally unmoved by the needs of others. Limited sympathy is not the same as lack of sympathy. This is a point Hume is at pains to emphasise in his account of the circumstances of justice:

> I am sensible, that generally speaking, the representations of this quality have been carried much too far; and that the descriptions, which certain philosophers delight so much to form of mankind in this particular, are as wide of nature as any accounts of monsters, which we meet with in fables and romances. So far from thinking, that men have no affection for any thing beyond themselves, I am of opinion, that though it be rare to meet with one, who loves any single person better than himself; yet it is as rare to meet with one, in whom all the kind affections, taken together, do not overbalance all the selfish.
>
> (Hume, 1896 [1739], pp.486–487)

Hume's affirmation of the kind affections may not go far enough: it is arguably not at all rare to meet people who love specific individuals (their children, for example) better than they love themselves. But his general point is clear: far from it being a hard fact of life that human beings are incurably self-interested, it is a manifest falsehood.

What, then, does it mean to say that our capacity for sympathy is limited? Simply that we are not so constituted as to be capable of caring as much about most other people as we do about ourselves and our loved ones. No doubt we are capable of some fellow feeling with all human beings, and of quite deep compassion for the suffering of people we do not know; but fellow feeling is a pale shadow of self-love and familial love, and our compassion for strangers in peril does not compare in intensity with the desperation we feel when the danger is to us or our children.

While we are by no means purely self-interested, we are undeniably somewhat self-interested, and in circumstances of want our desire to meet our own needs is characteristically stronger than our desire to meet the needs of others. As Warnock has it,

> A man who does not like being hungry, and who is naturally inclined to take such steps as he can to satisfy his hunger, may very well care less, even not at all, about the hunger of others, and may not care at all whether anything is done to satisfy them.
>
> *(Warnock, 1971, p.21)*

The point is not that the man in Warnock's example is generally insensible to the misfortunes of others, but rather that, in the throes of his own hunger, his determination to find food leaves little psychological room for altruistic concern.

And where we do have room for altruism, we allocate it disproportionately in favour of the people we love, or to whom we stand in some familial or tribal relationship. Our personal attachments and affiliations reduce the scope of our sympathy, or at least significantly distort its distribution. Having marvelled at the selflessness of love between family members, Hume ruefully observes that such love can be as inimical to the common good as pure self-interest:

> But though this generosity must be acknowledged to the honour of human nature, we may at the same time remark, that so noble an affection, instead of fitting men for large societies, is almost as contrary to them, as the most narrow selfishness.
>
> *(Hume, 1896 [1739], p.487)*

Again, limited sympathy is a contingent phenomenon. These are facts about our psychological makeup that might have been otherwise. But they are facts nonetheless.

The final circumstance of justice is moderate scarcity of resources. Human beings need, most basically, food, shelter and clothing; and they want, in addition, a wide range of natural resources and manufactured goods that can be acquired through individual or collective industry. But resources and goods are not so abundant that everyone's needs and wants can be easily met, or even met at all. At least in the case of the things people want, it seems certain that demand will always outstrip supply. There are numerous goods that all or many of us desire but not all or many of us can have, with the result that we are bound to find ourselves either envying what others possess or being envied for what we possess, and frequently both.

Moreover, few of the resources we need and want are simply there for the taking, provided by nature in just the form we need or want them. Their acquisition involves many kinds of human toil: sowing, harvesting, milling and baking; mining, smelting, forging and welding; felling, planing, treating and joining; and myriad more. So demanding and diverse is the work involved in generating the resources we require that none of us can expect to provide for ourselves without assistance. Just to be adequately fed, sheltered and clothed, let alone to enjoy the benefits of cars, computers and contact lenses, we need to work together, to cooperate in the organisation of tasks and the division of labour.

Importantly, however, the scarcity of resources and the difficulty of acquiring them is only moderate. Our situation is not such that, no matter what we do, large numbers of people must perish from exposure or starvation. The soil is not so barren, nor the climate so intemperate, that crops can be grown for only a few. We have at least a fighting chance of growing and making enough to go round, of meeting everyone's needs and some of their wants, even if not as many of their wants as we would like.

Rawls sums up the 'condition of moderate scarcity' like this:

> Natural and other resources are not so abundant that schemes of cooperation become superfluous, nor are conditions so harsh that fruitful ventures must inevitably break down. While mutually advantageous arrangements are feasible, the benefits they yield fall short of the demands men put forward.
>
> (Rawls, 1971, p.127)

This too might have been otherwise. We can imagine a world in which resources were not scarce or hard-won, in which nature provided amply and immediately for all our needs and wants. And we can imagine our needs and wants being other and simpler than they are. Hume invites us to consider the sheep and the ox, creatures with no need of shelter or clothing and the most undemanding of dietary requirements. But, contingently, that is not how things are for us. Our needs and wants are extensive and the means of satisfying them both moderately scarce and difficult to secure.

These, then, are the three features of the human condition that give rise to the problem of sociality. It is perhaps not difficult to see why their combination is a recipe for trouble. Because we are roughly equal in strength and intelligence, we each know that we have a reasonable chance of coming out on top in any physical or strategic conflict, and we are each aware that those around us know the same thing about their chances. Because our sympathy for strangers is limited, in the sense of being notably weaker than self-love and familial love, we are inclined to prioritise the safety and satisfaction of ourselves and our loved ones over the safety and satisfaction of others. And because resources are not abundant enough to satisfy everyone's needs and wants, we are forced into competition with each other for access to goods in short supply. The clear implication of these circumstances, taken together, is that there is, in human social groups, a *standing propensity to outbreaks of conflict*. Hobbes explains the propensity as follows:

> From this equality of ability, ariseth equality of hope in the attaining of our Ends. And therefore if any two men desire the same thing, which never-thelesse they cannot both enjoy, they become enemies; and in the way to their End, (which is principally their owne conservation, and sometimes their

delectation only,) endeavour to destroy, or subdue one an other. And from hence it comes to passe, that where an Invader hath no more to feare, than an other mans single power; if one plant, sow, build, or possesse a convenient Seat, others may probably be expected to come prepared with forces united, to dispossesse, and deprive him, not only of the fruit of his labour, but also of his life, or liberty. And the Invader again is in the like danger of another.

(Hobbes, 1929 [1651], p.95)

In a famous passage, Hobbes goes on to describe the fate of social groups in which the propensity to outbreaks of conflict is allowed to go unchecked:

In such condition, there is no place for Industry; because the fruit thereof is uncertain; and consequently no Culture of the Earth; no Navigation, nor use of the commodities that may be imported by Sea; no commodious Building; no Instruments of moving, and removing such things as require much force; no Knowledge of the face of the Earth; no account of Time; no Arts; no Letters; no Society; and which is worst of all, continuall feare, and danger of violent death; And the life of man, solitary, poore, nasty, brutish, and short.

(ibid., pp.96–97)

Hobbes focuses on physical conflict and the threat of violence, but perhaps equally perilous to human safety is strategic conflict and the threat of being out-manoeuvred in the competition for resources. Human beings have many more ways of depriving each other of the things they need than by the exercise of brute force. The war of everyone against everyone can be waged at least as effectively in legislative chambers and board rooms as it can on battlefields and isolated homesteads.

We are led into conflict with one another not merely by a desire to secure the things we need by fair means or foul, but by our awareness of this desire in others and our consequent distrust of them – what Hobbes calls 'diffidence'. We cannot be confident that others will not try to harm us, deceive us or otherwise deprive us of the fruit of our labour. And this makes it prudent for us to strike first, on the basis that attack is the best form of defence. It is diffidence, as much as competitiveness, that nudges us all too easily into a state of war. Diffidence has another unwelcome consequence too: it significantly impedes our ability to cooperate. The scarcity of resources and the difficulty of securing them makes cooperation vital if our needs are to be met and our wants satisfied; but cooperation depends on our being able to trust that everyone will perform the tasks allocated to them. Mackie describes the reasoning of those who lack this trust:

Your corn is ripe today; mine will be so tomorrow. It is profitable for us both that I should labour with you today, and that you should aid me tomorrow. I have no kindness for you, and know you have as little for me. I will not, therefore, take any pains upon your account; and should I labour with you upon my own account, in expectation of a return, I know I should be disappointed, and that I should in vain depend upon your gratitude. Here, then, I leave you to labour alone: you treat me in the same manner. The seasons change; and both of us lose our harvests for want of mutual confidence and security.

(Mackie, 1977, pp.110–111)

If we cannot be confident that others will play their parts in a cooperative scheme, it will be imprudent for us to dedicate too much time and energy to our own parts. We must assume that the scheme will founder and focus our efforts on the resources we can secure without assistance. Here diffidence has not necessarily brought us into conflict; it has merely prevented us from entering into cooperative arrangements or given us a reason to exit them. So the implication of rough equality, limited sympathy and moderate scarcity of resources is that human social groups have a standing propensity not only to outbreaks of conflict, but also to *breakdowns in cooperation*.

Some situations in which cooperation would be beneficial exhibit the features of a 'prisoner's dilemma', whereby it will always appear to a self-interested individual trying to anticipate the actions of those with whom she might cooperate that she is better off not cooperating. In the original model for situations of this kind, two criminals, guilty of a serious crime but held on evidence strong enough to convict them only of a petty one, are each invited to testify against the other. Collectively, their best bet is to cooperate with each other by refusing to testify and accepting short sentences for the petty crime. But, individually, it looks to each as though testifying is the smarter move. Criminal A knows that criminal B will either testify or refuse to testify. If B testifies, A should testify too: otherwise she alone will be convicted of the serious crime and her sentence will be long. But if B refuses to testify, A should still testify, because then she will go free while B is convicted. Testifying appears to offer A the best outcome regardless of what B does, and vice versa. So A and B are rationally motivated not to cooperate with each other, despite the fact that neither would be convicted of the serious crime if they did cooperate.

Certainly there are situations in life that have the structure of a prisoner's dilemma, and the fact that self-interested reasoning in these situations makes it appear imprudent to cooperate may be a contributing factor in some breakdowns of cooperation. But we should resist the temptation to make too much of cases like this. Most situations in which cooperation would be collectively beneficial are not prisoner's dilemmas: it may be generally imprudent for individuals to make cooperative arrangements with people likely to renege on them, but it is not generally imprudent for them to honour agreements with people prepared to do likewise. Mackie's farmer declines to help his neighbour because he believes that his help will not be reciprocated; if he could be reasonably confident of reciprocation, helping would be the prudent thing to do. It is only when the cost of cooperating is very high, or the benefit of not cooperating very great (as in the case of a criminal who can avoid jail time by testifying), that self-interested reasoning may seem to favour reneging on agreements with reliable others.

Moreover, we do not usually reason in the purely self-interested way assumed by the prisoner's dilemma. Our sympathy with others may be limited, but it is rarely absent. Other things being equal, we want those with whom we enter into cooperative arrangements to benefit from those arrangements in the same way we do. The prisoner's dilemma looks a little different if we assume that the two criminals care for each other and prefer to spare each other long sentences. And it is rather odd that Mackie's neighbouring farmers feel no kindness for one another: if they did, they would see value in giving assistance as well as receiving it. When weighing up the advantages and disadvantages of participating in a cooperative endeavour, we normally count among its advantages the benefits that accrue to others, not just the benefits that accrue to ourselves.

But if most situations are *not* prisoner's dilemmas, and most reasoning is *not* purely self-interested, why should we think that cooperation will tend to break down? Why should people not be confident enough in one another's good sense and goodwill to play their parts in cooperative schemes? The answer, of course, is that, although we can increase the resources available to us by cooperating, we must still compete with each other for those in short supply; and although we characteristically prefer that the needs of others are met, it matters rather more to us that our own needs are met. So we are continually prey to the temptation to default on cooperative arrangements when there is competitive advantage in doing so. And because we know that others are prey to the same temptation, we cannot assume that the arrangements will deliver the intended goods, which gives us further reason to default on them.

The problem of sociality, then, is the standing propensity in human social groups to breakdowns in cooperation and outbreaks of conflict, arising from the contingent but permanent circumstances of rough equality, limited sympathy and moderate scarcity of resources. And the most effective way for us to tackle this problem is to subscribe to some basic moral standards.

A justification for basic moral standards

There are straightforward practical reasons, both prudential and altruistic, for most of us, most of the time, to cooperate with each other and refrain from harming each other. Unfortunately, as we have just seen, these reasons are not sufficient to the task of sustaining cooperation and averting conflict. Self-interest and sympathy alone do not reliably yield peace and productivity. What we need is a supplementary kind of motivation for keeping to cooperative agreements and treating each other in non-harmful ways. We need the kind of motivation that subscription to standards can provide.

Recall that subscribing to a standard consists in intending to comply with it, feeling good about complying with it and bad about failing to comply with it, and being in the habit of complying with it. This syndrome of dispositions, attached to conflict-averting and cooperation-sustaining standards of conduct, can make up the motivational shortfall when our interests run counter to those of others and our sympathies run low. If I subscribe to a standard that prohibits stealing, I shall be disinclined to deprive my neighbour of the fruit of his labour even if I have no affection for him, could overpower or outrun him, and am confident that no one else would come to his aid.

But the problem of sociality will not be solved or ameliorated by subscription to conflict-averting and cooperation-sustaining standards unless *everyone*, or almost everyone, subscribes to them. Indeed, if only some people subscribe, the problem may actually be exacerbated. If some members of a social group commit themselves to prohibitions on theft and violence and other members do not, the former succeed only in making themselves more attractive targets to the latter. Similarly, if some parties to a cooperative scheme assume an obligation to perform the tasks allocated to them and other parties to the scheme do not, the temptation for the latter to free-ride on the hard work of the former may be all the greater. Even if the problem of sociality is not actually worsened by the subscription of some but not others, it is plain that little has been done to ameliorate it.

What the problem calls for, then, is not just subscription to the relevant standards of conduct, but universally-enlisting and penalty-endorsing subscription to them. We must each take responsibility not only for complying with the standards ourselves, but for actively encouraging others to comply and for standing ready to punish them when they do not. We must each do our bit to ensure that the standards have currency in society, that their authority is recognised by everyone. Without this, we cannot overcome the diffidence or distrust that arises from our awareness of the equal strength, limited sympathy and competitiveness of others. Only if we know that others intend and incline to cooperate with us and refrain from harming us can we trust them enough to make peaceful and productive social relations possible.

Moreover, our subscription to the relevant standards must be stringent. We must be sufficiently motivated to comply with them that we are able to resist the temptations of self-interest and the admonitions of distrust. So powerful are these temptations and admonitions that we sometimes need more motivational help with compliance than is provided by the prospect of feeling bad about non-compliance. We need the additional help of seeing our non-compliance as liable to punishment.

Effectively tackling the problem of sociality therefore requires not just subscription to conflict-averting and cooperation-sustaining standards of conduct, but *moral* subscription to them. It requires the kind of subscription that is concerned with the regulation of other people's conduct as well as one's own, and that is stringent enough to motivate compliance in the face of strong countervailing desires and inclinations. The distinguishing features of moral subscription, the features that make it peculiarly hard to justify in other circumstances, are precisely what make it adequate to the job of protecting human social groups against their standing propensity to breakdowns in cooperation and outbreaks of conflict.

Which standards of conduct are the conflict-averting and cooperation-sustaining ones? They are, unsurprisingly, the basic moral standards to which almost everyone does, in fact, subscribe. This is unsurprising because most people live in stable social groups and, ex hypothesi, social groups are not stable unless their members morally subscribe to conflict-averting and cooperation-sustaining standards. The standards include prohibitions on killing and causing harm, stealing and extorting, lying and cheating, and requirements to treat others fairly, keep one's promises and help those in need. To deal with the danger to each person of others coming 'to dispossesse, and deprive him, not only of the fruit of his labour, but also of his life, or liberty', there must be standards that afford basic protection to people and their property; and to overcome the distrust that threatens to make us 'lose our harvests for want of mutual confidence and security', there must be standards that oblige us to be fair, honest and reliable in our dealings with each other, and to extend each other a helping hand in times of need.

These are the moral standards we need to cope with the features of the human condition from which the problem of sociality arises. If the features were different, the standards needed to cope with them might be different too. Indeed, if the features were very different, subscription to moral standards might not be needed at all. This is a point emphasised by Hume:

> [The poets] easily perceived, if every man had tender regard for another, or if nature supplied abundantly all our wants and desires, that the jealousy of interest, which justice supposes, could no longer have place; nor would there be any occasion for those distinctions and limits of property and possession, which at present are in use among mankind. Encrease to a sufficient degree the benevolence of men, or the bounty of nature, and you render justice useless, by supplying its place with much nobler virtues, and more valuable blessings. The selfishness of men is animated by the few possessions we have, in proportion to our wants; and it is to restrain this selfishness, that men have been obliged to separate themselves from the community, and to distinguish betwixt their own goods and those of others.
>
> *(Hume, 1896 [1739], pp.494–495)*

It is not only an *increase* in the benevolence of men or the bounty of nature that would change things. So would a significant *decrease* in benevolence or bounty. If our sympathy for others were not just limited but non-existent, and we were motivated solely by self-interest, the case for subscribing to standards 'whose central task is to protect the interests of persons other than the agent' (Mackie, 1977, p.106) might look rather less compelling. And if resources were so scarce that there were no hope of meeting everyone's need for food, shelter and clothing, it might be harder to see why we should undertake to be fair, or honest, or to help those in need. So the problem-of-sociality justification for subscription to basic moral standards does not hold for all conceivable rational beings in all conceivable circumstances; it holds specifically for rational beings like us, living together under circumstances of rough equality, limited sympathy and moderate scarcity of resources.

Granted this restriction on its scope, however, the justification is sound. It does give us, situated as we are, a decisively good reason to subscribe to conflict-averting and cooperation-sustaining moral standards. We can have confidence, and teach children with confidence, that at least these moral standards are vindicated by at least this justificatory argument.

Two points are worth emphasising here. First, most of us subscribe to a wider set of moral standards than the handful needed to ameliorate the problem of sociality. We may hold ourselves and others to standards of service or redistribution that are much more demanding than the stability of social groups requires; or to standards of sexual conduct that have nothing to do with averting conflict or sustaining cooperation; or to standards that afford protection to entities other than human beings, such as non-human animals. Holding, and teaching, that basic moral standards are justified by the problem-of-sociality argument carries no implication that people do not or should not also subscribe to additional moral standards of these and other kinds.

Second, recognising that the problem-of-sociality justification is sound is quite compatible with believing that some other putative justification for subscribing to moral standards is also sound. It is no part of the foregoing argument that this is the *only* kind of good reason we could have for universally-enlisting and penalty-endorsing subscription to standards. It may turn out to be the case that basic moral standards are justified *both* by their capacity to avert conflict and sustain cooperation in human social groups *and*, say, by their divine authorisation, or by an imperative of pure practical reason to treat people as ends-in-themselves. Different justifications for the same standards can sit quite happily alongside each other; acceptance of one does not necessitate rejection of all others. The only advantage I am claiming for the problem-of-sociality justification is that, unlike other justificatory attempts, it is not a matter of reasonable disagreement among reasonable people. It is beyond serious dispute that human beings must contend with the problem of sociality, and that they can and do ameliorate that problem by subscribing to basic moral standards.

Nihilists, free-riders and the infirm

Justifications for morality of this kind are sometimes described as 'contractarian', on the grounds that undertaking to comply with a moral code in the expectation that others will do likewise is in some ways akin to making a contract with those others. The description is, of course, metaphorical. No actual contract is drawn up and there is no historical moment of negotiation and agreement. But it is true that justifications of this kind have a reciprocal or quid pro quo aspect that assumes tacit agreement among the members of a social group. Hume characterises the agreement as follows:

> I observe, that it will be for my interest to leave another in the possession of his goods, provided he will act in the same manner with regard to me. He is

sensible of a like interest in the regulation of his conduct. When this common sense of interest is mutually expressed, and is known to both, it produces a suitable resolution and behaviour. And this may properly enough be called a convention or agreement betwixt us, though without the interposition of a promise; since the actions of each of us have a reference to those of the other, and are performed upon the supposition that something is to be performed on the other part ... And it is only on the expectation of this, that our moderation and abstinence are founded.

(Hume, 1896 [1739], p.490)

As noted above, the problem of sociality is not ameliorated unless everyone, or almost everyone, subscribes to the relevant standards of conduct. So it is only rational for me to commit myself to complying with those standards if I have a reasonable expectation that everyone else will comply with them too. Of course, this is not merely a matter of prediction: I take active steps to bring about the compliance of others by enlisting their support for the standards and endorsing penalties for their non-compliance. But, still, my enlisting and endorsing would come to nought if others were not independently inclined to comply, and it is only because I take them to be so inclined that my own subscription is justified.

There are some standard objections to contractarian justifications for morality. Contractarianism comes in different shapes and sizes and the standard objections have more force against some varieties than others. In what remains of this chapter I shall try to show that they have little or no force against the justification for morality advanced above.

Objections to contractarianism focus on three types of people who are each thought to pose a threat to the justificatory enterprise: nihilists, free-riders and the infirm. Nihilists are lovers of chaos and conflict for whom the problem of sociality is not a problem at all and who therefore have no interest in the solution morality offers. Free-riders are people who care about the problem of sociality and see that it is ameliorated by the currency of moral standards, but think this gives them reason only to *feign* subscription to those standards, thereby securing the benefits of other people's compliance without incurring the costs of their own. And the infirm are those with diminished mental or physical capacities who pose no significant threat to others in a social group and who are therefore at risk of being excluded from the contract and exempted from moral protection. Let us consider each of these types in turn.

The first and most obvious thing to say about nihilists is that they probably don't exist. They are in large part a figment of the philosophical imagination. It is probably true that *if* people were so constituted as to care nothing for their own safety and sustenance, or the safety and sustenance of their families, *then* they would be untroubled by the standing propensity of human social groups to breakdowns in cooperation and outbreaks of conflict. But that is not how people are constituted. Both the problem of sociality and its solution rest on an account of what human beings are actually like: their mental and physical capacities, their self-love and sympathy for others, their need for food, shelter and clothing, their readiness both to compete and to cooperate. It is no part of the view defended here that the justification for morality would continue to hold through any conceivable change in our psychological makeup.

The most basic assumption about human beings underpinning the problem of sociality is that they wish to survive. The argument does not purport to justify the desire for survival, but takes it as a premise from which reasons for subscribing to moral standards can be derived. Hart argues that 'the modest aim of survival' is 'the central indisputable element' that can be rescued from older theories of natural law:

> we can, in referring to survival, discard, as too metaphysical for modern minds, the notion that this is something antecedently fixed which men necessarily desire because it is their proper goal or end. Instead we may hold it to be a mere contingent fact which could be otherwise, that in general men do desire to live, and that we may mean nothing more by calling survival a human goal or end than that men do desire it. Yet even if we think of it in this common-sense way, survival still has a special status in relation to human conduct and in our thought about it … For it is not merely that an overwhelming majority of men do wish to live, even at the cost of hideous misery, but that this is reflected in whole structures of our thought and language, in terms of which we describe the world and each other. We could not subtract the general wish to live and leave intact concepts like danger and safety, harm and benefit, need and function, disease and cure; for these are ways of simultaneously describing and appraising things by reference to the contribution they make to survival which is accepted as an aim.
>
> (Hart, 1994 [1961], pp.191–192)

It is precisely because human beings are not nihilists, do not love chaos and conflict, but rather want to survive, and to live in safety and comfort, that the problem of sociality is a pressing one for them. If the question is 'But what if people were otherwise?' the answer is 'Then their problems would be otherwise and subscription to moral standards may not solve them. But so what?' Basic moral standards are justified because they answer to the needs of real human beings; whether they also answer to the needs of fictional ones has no bearing on the matter.

Perhaps there are a few benighted souls in the world who *are* nihilists in the relevant sense, who really do relish destruction and disregard their own and others' survival. If so, it is surely right to say that the problem-of-sociality justification for subscription to moral standards will be unpersuasive to them. They are unlikely to be willing parties to the tacit agreement on which morality rests. As long as such people are in a small minority, however, their existence does not deprive the rest of us of the good reason we have to be moral. Amelioration of the problem of sociality requires all *or nearly all* members of a social group to subscribe to conflict-averting and cooperation-sustaining standards of conduct. A small number of resolute non-subscribers, while they certainly pose a threat to peace and productivity, can be contained and managed by the community of subscribers, either by finding alternative ways to motivate compliance or by curbing freedom so as to prevent or mitigate the effects of non-compliance. As long as we can reasonably expect that *most* others will see the sense in subscribing, it will be sensible for us to subscribe too. Only if nihilists existed in large numbers would they represent a serious challenge to the problem-of-sociality justification; and it seems plain that they do not.

Unlike nihilists, free-riders are as worried as the rest of us about the trouble caused by rough equality, limited sympathy and moderate scarcity of resources. And they agree that the currency in society of basic moral standards is an effective way to address the problem. They see why there should be penalties for non-compliance with these standards and are ready to play their part in admonishing and punishing those who violate them. But they deny that any of this requires them to have the syndrome of attitudes and dispositions in which moral subscription consists. All it requires is an ability to feign those attitudes and dispositions, to convince others that they intend and incline to comply with moral standards, while actually being willing to violate them whenever their interests are served by doing so and the chances of detection are low. In this way they can enjoy the benefits of living in a community of moral subscribers without having to pay the costs of subscription themselves.

Free-riders, then, are less fanciful creatures, less psychologically remote from ordinary human beings, than nihilists, and in this sense pose more of a threat to contractarian justifications of morality. It looks as though the option of feigning subscription to moral standards is a live one for members of social groups and, as long as only a few of them take up the option, one that is unlikely to be too damaging to the project of ameliorating the problem of sociality. The danger, of course, is that this line of reasoning might prove attractive to more than a few. If large numbers of people were to be persuaded of the case for free-riding, the tacit agreement on which morality rests would break down and moral subscription would cease to be rational for anyone. So we need to know why we should neither free-ride ourselves nor be dissuaded from moral subscription by the free-riding of others.

One thing to be said to those tempted to free-ride is the point just made: if everyone free-rides, the moral system collapses. This is true, and relevant, but unlikely to be wholly persuasive. The would-be free-rider knows quite well that not everyone can free-ride, that the maxim 'feign subscription to moral standards' cannot be universalised. She understands that the course of action she is thinking about taking is dependent on others not taking it. Her question is whether, if she is confident in the moral subscription of others, her interests are better served by feigning subscription than by actually subscribing; and this is at least an intelligible question to ask.

Another thing to be said to the would-be free-rider is that feigning moral subscription may be rather more difficult than it first appears. To subscribe to moral standards is to have a stable set of conative, affective and behavioural dispositions, to be the sort of person who intends to conduct herself in a certain way, habitually does conduct herself in that way, and feels ashamed of herself when she does not. Successfully convincing others that one is a person of that sort, when in fact one lacks these dispositions and is entirely at ease with conduct that violates the standards, is no mean feat. The pretence must be kept up more or less continuously and with more or less everyone, including those with whom one has intimate personal or familial relationships. To borrow terms from David Gauthier (1986), human beings may not be *transparent* (that is, such that their dispositions are fully and unmistakeably accessible to others), but they are at least *translucent* (that is, such that their dispositions are at least partially and defeasibly accessible to others). It is easy enough to pretend to be something one is not in a brief meeting with a stranger, but our translucency makes it difficult to maintain the illusion for long or with close acquaintances, let alone permanently and with all acquaintances. This is not to deny that feigning subscription to moral standards is possible, but rather to observe that the cost of doing so, in terms of the effort required to keep up the pretence, may be significantly higher than the cost of actually subscribing.

Still, it might be countered, it isn't self-evident that feigning subscription is costlier than subscribing, so if this is the strongest objection to free-riding, we cannot safely assume that everyone, or almost everyone, will be dissuaded from giving it a try. Fortunately, there is another, more basic reply to the free-rider problem that does allow us to assume this. Although free-riders are less fanciful creatures than nihilists, there is still one important respect in which they are psychologically remote from ordinary human beings: they are motivated purely by self-interest. Their practical reasoning is wholly prudential and not at all altruistic. The judgment they make, in choosing to free-ride, is that the benefits of violating moral standards undetected outweigh the costs of keeping up the pretence of subscribing to them. They simply leave out of account the costs of their violations to others. The suffering caused by their undetected lies, injuries and injustices does not enter into their thinking about the advantages and disadvantages of moral subscription. And this makes the free-rider at best a psychological oddity and at worst another figment of the philosophical imagination.

Actual human beings are sympathetic as well as self-interested. Their sympathy is limited, in the ways noted above, but it is a salient feature of their motivational set. And it plays an important role in the problem-of-sociality justification for morality. The good reason I have for subscribing to basic moral standards is that their currency in society makes life safer and easier for me *and everyone else*. Because I am strongly invested in my own welfare and at least somewhat invested in the welfare of others, the fact that everyone benefits from my moral subscription is a significant part of its rational appeal. My prudential and altruistic preferences are in alignment in my judgment that it makes sense to subscribe. The fundamental objection to merely feigning moral subscription is not that keeping up the pretence is difficult, nor that too many free-riders bring down the system, but that free-riding is only an attractive option to those unconcerned by the harmful impact of moral violations on others. And few, if any, people are like that.

The threat to contractarian justifications of morality posed by the infirm is of a rather different kind. The worry here is not so much about whether the problem-of-sociality justification succeeds as about what it succeeds in justifying. We have reason to hold ourselves and each other to moral standards because we are roughly equal in strength and intelligence and therefore represent a permanent danger to each other. But what of people who, for reason of mental or physical frailty, represent no danger to anyone? Harmless people need not be held to standards of conduct designed to prevent them from doing harm, and may be ill-equipped to play a role in holding others to those standards. So does it not make sense simply to exclude them from the metaphorical contract? If the infirm are not part of the problem of sociality, they need not be part of the solution either. They can be spared the obligations and denied the protections of morality.

The charge, then, is that the moral standards contractarianism justifies are not, after all, the basic moral standards to which more or less everyone currently subscribes, but a repugnant variation on them that denies protection to the most vulnerable members of society. The justified moral code is one that prohibits harming, stealing from and lying to people of ordinary strength and intelligence, but readily permits those things in relation to the infirm. It requires that we help those in need if the need is moderate and temporary, but not if the need is severe and permanent. If the objection holds, contractarianism gives us moral standards all right, but not the ones we want.

Two replies to this objection are jointly sufficient to defeat it. The first is that it assumes much too sharp a line between people of ordinary strength and intelligence and the infirm. For a moral standard to specify an obligation to people of the first kind but not those of the second, there would need to be some straightforward way of sorting people into these two groups; but there is no such way. For one thing, there are many kinds of infirmity, so a person may be incapable of causing some kinds of harm but still quite adequately equipped to cause others. For another thing, many infirmities are temporary, so the fact that someone poses no threat in the present does not mean she will pose no threat in the future. Moreover, our ability to assess levels of infirmity in others is limited: it is easy to be wrong about the powers and frailties of the people we encounter. Recall that the notion of rough equality on which the problem of sociality rests explicitly recognises that there is wide variation in people's mental and physical capacities. The point is that, notwithstanding this variation, the difference between the strong and the weak is never so great as to render the discontent of the latter irrelevant to the fortunes of the former. These practical and prudential considerations count against any attempt to exclude the infirm from the sphere of moral obligation and protection.

The second, and stronger, reply is the by-now-familiar point that this objection ignores human sympathy and the altruistic reasons for subscribing to moral standards. If the *only* reasons we had for subscribing were self-interested ones, and we really *could* identify people whose exclusion from morality was entirely without risk, then perhaps it would be rational to exclude them. But, crucially, this is not how things are. We care for other people, sympathise with their difficulties and feel compassion for their suffering. We want *everyone* to be protected by the currency of moral standards in society, not least those most vulnerable to harm and exploitation by others. Our altruistic concern for the young, the sick and the elderly is keenly felt and central to the rational appeal of moral subscription. If, by holding ourselves and each other to moral standards, we can make the world a safer place for those ill-equipped to fend for themselves, that alone may be reason enough to do so – and it is certainly reason enough when combined with the prudential benefits of living in a morally regulated society. Excluding the infirm from the scope of our moral standards would simply render them unfit for purpose.

I conclude that the challenges posed by nihilists, free-riders and the infirm to the problem-of-sociality justification for morality can be satisfactorily answered. In answering them I have relied heavily on the important psychological fact about human beings that they are sympathetic to one another. Some contractarian justificatory theories try to avoid reliance on this fact: Gauthier, for example, builds his contractarian theory on an assumption of 'mutual unconcern' (Gauthier, 1986). This is a theoretical constraint that makes the task of justifying morality much more difficult, perhaps insurmountably so, and it is quite unnecessary. The foregoing justification rests on a realistic, not a pessimistic, account of the human condition. Given the combination of self-interested and sympathetic concerns human beings actually have, the case for tackling the problem of sociality by holding ourselves and each other to basic moral standards is compelling.

6

RATIONAL MORAL EDUCATION

I suggested at the beginning of this book that the problem for moral education posed by reasonable disagreement about morality consists in the difficulty of reconciling three claims:

1. Moral education aims to bring it about that children subscribe to moral standards and believe them to be justified.
2. There is reasonable disagreement about the content and justification of morality.
3. Teaching propositions as true, or standards as justified, when there is reasonable disagreement about them, is indoctrinatory.

We are now in a position to see the way out of this apparent impasse. While it is certainly true that there is reasonable disagreement about the content and justification of morality, it is not true that no moral standards are robustly justified. Reasonable disagreement about morality does not go all the way down. Some basic moral standards to which almost everyone currently subscribes enjoy the support of a decisive justificatory argument. Moral educators can properly aim to bring it about that children subscribe to these standards and believe them to be justified; and they can realise this aim without resorting to anything that resembles indoctrination. Teaching for full moral commitment to conflict-averting and cooperation-sustaining standards is quite consistent with the demands of reason.

Armed with a solution to our central problem, I should like in this chapter to sketch the contours of a rational scheme of moral education. My proposal is that the domain of moral standards and justificatory arguments should be divided into three groups, and that different pedagogical aims are appropriate to each. The first group comprises justified moral standards and sound justificatory arguments: here the pedagogical aim is to cultivate full moral commitment through a combination of moral formation and directive moral inquiry. The second group comprises moral standards and justificatory arguments whose status and soundness are matters of reasonable disagreement: in this case the appropriate pedagogy is nondirective moral inquiry, aimed at equipping children to form their own considered views. The third group comprises unjustified moral standards and unsound justificatory arguments, for which the appropriate pedagogy is a form of directive moral inquiry that discourages allegiance to the standards and arguments in question. Let us consider each of these groups and associated aims in turn.

Teaching justified moral standards

Where moral standards are robustly justified we should teach for full moral commitment to them. We should bring it about that children subscribe to them by means of moral formation; and we should bring it about that children believe them to be justified by means of directive moral inquiry.

As described in Chapter Three, moral formation is the cultivation in children of the conative, affective and behavioural dispositions that constitute subscription to moral standards. Its chief methods are the issuing of prescriptions, the rewarding of compliance, the punishing of non-compliance, the modelling of compliance, and the modelling of reactions to the compliance and non-compliance of others. These ways of shaping children's intentions, feelings and habits are supplemented by efforts to improve their thinking about the application of their standards.

Moral inquiry is inquiry into whether and how moral standards are justified. It involves investigating the nature of moral standards, asking what might justify subscription to such standards, and examining the strength of suggested justifications. Moral inquiry is directive when there is a deliberate attempt to persuade children that a standard is, or is not, justified. Directive moral inquiry may be didactic or nondidactic or a mixture of the two.

That we are entitled to teach for full moral commitment to justified moral standards should be clear enough. Here we are shaping children's dispositions and guiding their beliefs in accordance with the demands of reason. We are both equipping them with traits they would choose to have if they were choosing rationally and helping them to see why they would choose those traits.

It should also be clear that we are *only* entitled to teach children to believe that moral standards are justified when they really are justified. Getting children to believe standards to be justified when they are not, or when their justificatory status is a matter of reasonable disagreement, is indoctrinatory because it necessarily involves the use of non-rational means of persuasion. The available justificatory arguments are unsuccessful or inconclusive, so must be supplemented with some form of manipulation or psychological pressure to secure the desired belief. And to impart beliefs to children by such means is to do them cognitive harm.

It is less obvious that we are only entitled to teach for subscription to moral standards when the standards in question are justified; but I want to defend that claim too. The cultivation of conative, affective and behavioural dispositions cannot itself be indoctrinatory because these are not the sorts of things that can be indoctrinated: worries about indoctrination pertain specifically to the teaching of beliefs. But that does not give parents and teachers carte blanche to shape children's intentions, feelings and habits in any way they please. John Wilson may be right that the unindoctrinated mind remains free 'however much our behaviour may be forced or our feelings conditioned' (Wilson et al., 1967, p.174), but conditioning feelings and habituating patterns of behaviour are still significant interventions in children's lives with a lasting effect on the kinds of adults they become. It is important for educators to be clear about the range of dispositions they are trying to cultivate in children and on what grounds. When it comes to the dispositions that constitute moral subscription, I suggest, the most defensible educational principle is that children should be brought to subscribe only to moral standards for which there is a sound justification, and should be provided with that justification as soon as they are capable of grasping it.

There is another, more practical reason for restricting the content of moral formation to the class of justified moral standards. Although moral formation and directive moral inquiry are logically distinct and can be pursued independently of one another, it is in practice very difficult to pull them apart completely. As noted earlier, children will comply with prescriptions, accept punishments and emulate rule-following in the way moral formation requires, but they will also ask *why* the prescriptions are being issued, the punishments meted out and the rules followed, and will expect their questions to be satisfactorily answered. If we ignore or evade their questions we weaken their inclination to comply, accept and emulate and put the enterprise of moral formation in jeopardy. But if we are only entitled to teach children that moral standards are justified when they really are justified – that is, if we accept the suggested constraint on the content of directive moral inquiry – it is clear that we shall be compelled to accept a similar constraint on the content of moral formation. It will be impossible to give satisfactory answers to children's 'why' questions if the standards to which we are cultivating their subscription are unjustified or of uncertain justificatory status.

The class of justified moral standards includes, at a minimum, the conflict-averting and cooperation-sustaining standards whose currency in society is necessary to ameliorate the problem of sociality. It includes, that is to say, prohibitions on killing and causing harm, stealing and extorting, lying and cheating, and requirements to treat others fairly, keep one's promises and help those in need. These standards at least should be taught in such a way that children come to subscribe to them and believe them to be justified. I do not wish to rule out the possibility of there being more justified moral standards than these. Perhaps there are other standards whose currency in society is necessary to ameliorate the problem of sociality; or perhaps there are standards that play no role in ameliorating the problem of sociality but are vindicated by some other sound justificatory argument. If so, these standards too should be taught with a view to securing full moral commitment.

The formation and inquiry components of teaching for full moral commitment should be complementary and mutually reinforcing. Admonishing children for lying supports and is supported by explaining to them the reasons for the prohibition on lying. Sometimes a single intervention is designed both to admonish and to explain ('Don't you see that if you lie to me, I won't be able to trust you any more?'); sometimes the explanation comes shortly after the admonition, when tempers are less frayed and matters can be discussed calmly. Often, though, there is little temporal connection between moral formation and directive moral inquiry. The prescribing, rewarding, punishing and modelling by which subscription to moral standards is cultivated tend to be spontaneous, occurring as and when needed in the course of daily life, most commonly when moral standards have been breached or the temptation to breach them is strong. In contrast, the explicit teaching and guided discussions by which children come to understand the justification for morality tend to be planned, occurring at times identified by parents or teachers as conducive to reflection and inquiry.

The separation of moral formation and directive moral inquiry is particularly pronounced in schools. Teachers discharge their responsibility for the moral formation of children chiefly in disciplinary encounters – in their responses to incidents of fighting and bullying, stealing from lunch boxes, cheating on tests and lying about homework – and in such pastoral and community-building contexts as tutor group meetings and school assemblies, where there is an established place for moral exhortation and prescription. But these encounters and contexts afford little opportunity for sustained inquiry into the justification for morality. Directive moral inquiry, if it happens at all in schools, usually happens in the context of academic subject teaching, with its emphasis on exposition, exploration, reflection and discussion. To be sure, few schools currently offer a subject dedicated to the study of morality, but many find room for it in other subjects ostensibly focused on the study of religion, society, politics or health. The point here is that such provision as schools make for moral inquiry is typically quite separate from the provision they make for moral formation.

There is, moreover, a good pedagogical reason for keeping moral inquiry apart from moral formation at least some of the time. In order to think through the justification of basic moral standards it is necessary to recognise that subscribing to moral standards is something we can choose not to do, and to consider the possibility that it is something we have no reason to do. Moral scepticism must be theoretically entertained by anyone grappling with the question of justification. The aim of directive moral education is, of course, to refute such scepticism and persuade children that the case for subscribing to basic moral standards is compelling; but to take them on this journey we must first allow them to feel the force of the justificatory problem. And it is difficult to open up a theoretical space for children to entertain moral scepticism *at the same time* as trying to cultivate their subscription to moral standards by means of prescribing, rewarding and punishing. The measures by which children are brought to feel good about complying and bad about failing to comply with moral standards are at least in tension with the invitation to question the justification of those standards. The tension is psychological rather than logical: there is no formal incompatibility between the two endeavours. But it is easier for children to engage in serious inquiry about the nature and justification of morality if they can do so at one remove from the processes of conditioning and habituation by which their moral dispositions are formed.

Teaching controversial moral standards

Where the status of moral standards and the soundness of justificatory arguments are matters of reasonable disagreement, we should equip children to form their own considered views on those standards and arguments by means of nondirective moral inquiry. Moral inquiry is nondirective when no attempt is made to persuade children that a standard is, or is not, justified or that an argument is, or is not, sound.

Matters of reasonable disagreement should be taught nondirectively because the evidence and argument bearing on them is subject to more than one plausible interpretation. It is the responsibility of educators to bring to light the range of plausible interpretations and to help children assess their strengths and weaknesses. Inducing children to accept or reject any one interpretation would involve the use of non-rational means of persuasion and is therefore educationally impermissible.

Often, moral educators will themselves believe controversial moral standards to be justified and controversial justificatory arguments to be sound. Such beliefs are perfectly in order: confronted with a matter of reasonable disagreement, a responsible epistemic agent may choose either to remain agnostic or to adopt the interpretation of the available evidence and argument she finds most plausible. What educators must recognise, though, is that the evidential standards for belief adoption and belief transmission are different. It is one thing to choose for oneself from a range of plausible interpretations; quite another to choose for someone else. The entitlement to adopt a belief one judges to be marginally better supported than others by ambiguous evidence and argument does not imply an entitlement to transmit that belief to children. The onus is therefore on moral educators to consider which of their moral standards are robustly justified and which are of uncertain justificatory status, and to teach the latter nondirectively.

Nondirective moral inquiry, like its directive counterpart, may involve both didactic and nondidactic teaching methods, but will normally lean more heavily on the latter. There is certainly a role for instructing, informing and explaining in acquainting children with controversial moral standards and justificatory arguments; but insofar as the aim is to enable children to form their own considered views, the emphasis will be on exploration, investigation and discussion. Children must have opportunities to hear, weigh up and respond to the arguments for and against controversial moral standards. They must come to understand that these are questions to which authoritative answers are unavailable, and be given space to think and talk about the non-authoritative answers on offer. Nondidactic teaching methods will, on the whole, better enable children to work out where they stand on controversial moral standards and arguments than didactic ones.

In light of the claim that there is at least one sound justification for moral subscription, we may distinguish two ways in which moral standards can be controversial. First, it may be unclear whether or not a given moral standard belongs to the moral code vindicated by a sound justificatory argument. Second, a given moral standard may rest on a justificatory argument whose soundness is in doubt. It may help to give an example of each.

Some people endorse, and some people reject, a moral prohibition on smacking children. Suppose that at least some of the people who endorse it do so on the basis of the problem-of-sociality justification for basic moral standards. In order to avert conflict and sustain cooperation, we should all morally subscribe to standards that protect us from different forms of harm and deprivation at one another's hands; and among these standards is one that prohibits parents from smacking their children. Here the anti-smackers are invoking a sound justification for morality in support of their favoured prohibition: the question is whether the moral code justified really does include this prohibition.

It is easy to see why anti-smackers think it does. Smacking is certainly a form of violence, perpetrated by one person against another with the intention of causing pain. We readily count the vast majority of violent acts, and acts intended to cause pain, among the forms of harm against which morality is designed to protect us. So the view that a moral prohibition on smacking is justified is a plausible one. But there are also credible things to be said against this view. When a mother smacks a child for, say, tripping up his younger sister near the top of a staircase, or next to a busy road, it is plain that she is attempting to act in the best interests of both children. She is endeavouring to protect her daughter from future harm at her brother's hands; and she is attempting to convey to her son the seriousness of his wrongdoing and to establish in him a visceral aversion to putting others in danger. Although she intends to cause her son temporary pain, she does not intend to injure him or cause him harm. Her purposes are educative, and while it is not self-evident that smacking is an effective educational tool, nor is it self-evident that it is not. So it is also at least plausible to hold that smacking is a kind of violence against which the protection of morality is not required.

Now consider the controversial moral standard 'do not eat meat'. Few people who endorse this standard do so on the grounds that its currency in society ameliorates the problem of sociality. Whatever else may be wrong with it, the practice of killing and eating animals does not appear to threaten the stability of human social groups. The most familiar justificatory argument for a moral prohibition on meat-eating is the utilitarian one advanced by the likes of Peter Singer (Singer, 1975). On this view, moral vegetarianism is required by the principle of utility, which Mill formulates as follows:

> The creed which accepts as the foundation of morals, Utility, or the Greatest Happiness Principle, holds that actions are right in proportion as they tend to promote happiness, wrong as they tend to produce the reverse of happiness. By happiness is intended pleasure, and the absence of pain; by unhappiness, pain, and the privation of pleasure.
>
> *(Mill, 1962 [1861], p.257)*

Because animals are indubitably capable of experiencing pleasure and pain, the hedonic calculus must include the pleasure and pain felt by animals as well as the pleasure and pain felt by people. And, when we take the suffering of animals into account, it seems hard to deny that the quantity of pain caused by the meat industry comfortably outweighs the quantity of pleasure it generates.

What makes moral vegetarianism controversial is not, or not primarily, reasonable disagreement about whether the principle of utility requires it; it is reasonable disagreement about whether the utilitarian justification for subscription to moral standards is sound. That is to say, the case for universally-enlisting and penalty-endorsing subscription to any and all pleasure-producing and pain-reducing standards has not been decisively made. The goal of maximising the quantity of pleasure and minimising the quantity of pain in the world is a worthy one, to be sure. But, first, there are other worthy goals too; and, second, it is far from clear that this one is worthy enough to justify holding ourselves and others, on pain of punishment, to standards of conduct designed to further it.

The distinction, then, is between controversial standards like the prohibition on smacking, which invoke sound justificatory arguments but may fall outside their scope, and controversial standards like the prohibition on meat-eating, which invoke justificatory arguments that may not be sound. It is, of course, quite possible for standards to be controversial in both these ways. Children should be given opportunities to think and talk about both kinds of controversy, and educators should refrain from guiding them towards particular verdicts on the standards in question.

If the first task of moral education is to bring it about that children subscribe to moral standards and believe them to be justified, it might be wondered what value there is in teaching them about controversial moral standards and justificatory arguments at all. If, in teaching these controversies, we are making no attempt at moral formation or moral direction, what do children stand to gain from engaging with them? And, indeed, do we not risk weakening children's nascent commitment to justified moral standards if we complicate matters by drawing their attention to intractable disputes in moral theory?

The worry about unhelpfully complicating matters is, I think, a real one. An undue focus on controversial moral standards and justificatory arguments can certainly give children the impression that the moral domain is peculiarly difficult to navigate. Moral education programmes that put too much emphasis on debating divisive moral issues, or examining the strengths and weaknesses of competing moral theories, easily, if inadvertently, give succour to moral agnosticism, to the thought that everything is up for grabs in the marketplace of moral ideas.

But the solution to this problem is not to try to hide, disguise or downplay the extent of reasonable disagreement about morality: it is to teach controversial standards alongside justified ones, and controversial arguments alongside sound ones. As long as nondirective inquiry into the grey areas of morality is paired with directive inquiry into the black and white areas, there is no reason to fear that engaging with controversies will have a corrosive effect on children's commitment to basic moral standards. This is not to deny that entering the grey areas can be disorientating, or that moral educators need to give careful thought to exactly when and how children are introduced to moral disputes of different kinds; but it is to deny that the grey areas should be fenced off and circumvented in an effort to protect children from contamination.

And the positive reasons for teaching controversial moral standards and justificatory arguments are at least threefold. First, children are aware of and curious about moral disagreement. They are acquainted with people who have and people who do not have moral objections to smacking, or eating meat, or gambling, or terminating unwanted pregnancies. They want to know why people disagree about these matters and who is right. Harnessing this curiosity by giving children opportunities to explore and discuss moral controversies is an effective way of drawing them into the practice of moral inquiry and nurturing in them a proper concern for the justification of moral standards. Stamping on their curiosity by closing down opportunities for exploration and discussion is, by contrast, a surefire way of losing their interest.

Second, independently of children's curiosity about them, moral disagreements matter. The fact that some but not all people morally object to, say, the termination of unwanted pregnancies is a cause of significant social division and personal distress. To endorse a moral prohibition on abortion is necessarily to want and expect others to comply with it and to favour their being punished in some way for not complying with it. So there is bound to be some level of conflict between those whose moral codes permit abortion and those whose moral codes do not. Disagreement about the content of morality is in this sense a problem for the members of human social groups, and one they have a common interest in solving. Our task as educators is not just to share with the young the knowledge we have accumulated and the solutions we have found; we must also equip them to participate in the debates we have been unable to settle and take on the challenges we have been unable to meet.

And third, independently of either children's interest in them or the trouble they cause in society, moral disagreements are the lifeblood of moral inquiry. Any serious educational attempt to initiate children into the practice of moral inquiry must recognise both the existence of controversies and their role in generating new ideas, arguments and lines of criticism. In this respect, moral inquiry is no different from any other form of inquiry into which educators initiate children. Robert Dearden, discussing the place of controversial issues in the school curriculum, observes that 'to teach a subject in a way that makes no reference to the controversial parts of it is to misrepresent it' (Dearden, 1981, p.41). He continues:

> At the cutting edge of any subject, much, if not everything, will be controversial ... And it is not an idle luxury to appreciate this. It is essential to an adequate grasp of the nature of human inquiry, of its dependence on imaginative ideas, of the place of criticism in it, of its advancement sometimes by fruitful wrong ideas rather than by pedestrian right ones, and of its tools and standards.
>
> *(ibid.)*

Like all human inquiry, moral inquiry is driven forward by proposals and counter-proposals, speculation and disputation, argument and criticism. It was by these means that such justified moral standards and sound justificatory arguments as we now have were vindicated, and by these means that any future additions to the stock of justified standards and sound arguments will be made. Initiates into the practice of moral inquiry should therefore be acquainted with its controversies and conjectures as well as its achievements and certainties.

Teaching unjustified moral standards

Where moral standards are demonstrably not justified, we should discourage children from believing that they are. Unjustified moral standards, like justified ones, should be taught by means of directive moral inquiry; but here the directive aim is to persuade children *not* to believe them to be justified, or to relinquish such beliefs if already held. Again, directive moral inquiry with this aim may be didactic or nondidactic or a mixture of the two.

Up to this point I have had little to say about unjustified moral standards and unsound justificatory arguments. I have focused on the reasonable disagreement to which many moral standards and justificatory arguments are subject, and on the rational vindication of basic moral standards by the problem-of-sociality justification. I now want to suggest that there are some moral standards we cannot properly regard as either justified or of uncertain justificatory status, and some justificatory arguments we cannot properly regard as either sound or of uncertain soundness. There are, that is to say, some moral standards and justificatory arguments for which it is impossible to mount a plausible defence.

An example of a standard to which moral subscription is demonstrably not justified, despite the fact that some people do morally subscribe to it, is 'do not masturbate'. There is simply no plausible argument in support of a moral prohibition on masturbation. There is disagreement about the standard, but there is no *reasonable* disagreement about it. Each of us is at liberty to refrain from masturbation, and some of us may have good reasons for doing so; but none of us has a remotely good reason to hold everyone, on pain of punishment, to a standard that prohibits it.

An example of a justificatory argument that is demonstrably unsound, despite the fact that some people advance it in support of their moral standards, is the argument that something is morally permissible because it occurs 'naturally', or morally impermissible because it does not occur 'naturally'. One objection to this argument is that there is no non-arbitrary way of dividing the things people do into the categories 'natural' and 'unnatural'. Another objection is that, once this division has been made, there is no good reason to permit everything in the first category and prohibit everything in the second. Suppose one decides to count human behaviour as natural if it is also encountered in the animal world and as unnatural if not encountered there. Well, then all manner of benign human activities – programming computers, baking cakes, attending concerts – immediately qualify as unnatural, and all manner of nasty ones – infanticide, cannibalism and killing for sport – qualify as natural. Patently, such a distinction affords no basis for a moral code of conduct.

There are, then, some moral standards and justificatory arguments that are rationally indefensible. To endorse a moral prohibition on masturbation, or to defend one's moral standards by appeal to what is natural, is to make an intellectual error. It is to exhibit a failure to be guided by reason in the moral sphere. And where moral standards are known to be unjustified, or justificatory arguments known to be unsound, there is an obvious prima facie case for teaching them as such. Teaching about unjustified standards and unsound arguments should have the aim of bringing it about that children see what is wrong with them and so refrain from endorsing them.

Now consider an objection to this prima facie case. It might be suggested that, in open and plural societies, directive moral teaching should be kept to a minimum. Because social stability depends on general subscription to conflict-averting and cooperation-sustaining moral standards, directive moral inquiry cannot be avoided altogether: we can and should bring it about that children believe these standards to be justified. But beyond securing their endorsement of basic morality, we should strive to keep moral inquiry as open-ended as possible. There is no enduring human problem, comparable to the problem of sociality, whose solution consists in ensuring that people do not endorse unjustified moral standards. So unjustified standards and unsound arguments should be taught in the same way as controversial standards and arguments: by means of nondirective moral inquiry, aimed at equipping children to form their own considered views.

One reply to this objection is that, while adherence to unjustified moral standards does not cause difficulties on the same scale as non-adherence to justified moral standards, nor is it unproblematic. Children raised to believe that masturbation is morally wrong may not pose an immediate threat to anyone's safety, but they are frequently encumbered with years of needless guilt or frustration. And because unjustified moral standards are rarely endorsed by all members of a social group, they tend to be socially divisive in the same way as controversial moral standards: attempts by subscribers to penalise the non-compliance of non-subscribers are not usually well received. In this sense subscription to unjustified moral standards is at least somewhat troublesome, and educational efforts to discourage it do promise to help.

A more basic reply to the objection, though, is that there is no warrant for the implied principle that moral teaching should be nondirective in the absence of a pressing social need for it to be directive. Certainly that principle would not be accepted in other areas of teaching. Incorrect solutions to mathematical problems, falsified scientific hypotheses and mistranslated German words are ordinarily taught as incorrect, falsified and mistranslated: few educators see merit in keeping inquiry open-ended in these cases, and that is surely not because they fear the dire social consequences of mathematical errors and mistranslations. They teach these things as incorrect because they are *known* to be incorrect, and because education is centrally concerned with the transmission of knowledge. Presumably, then, defenders of the principle think there is something peculiar to the moral domain that makes it desirable to refrain from transmitting such knowledge as we have about the status and soundness of standards and arguments unless absolutely necessary. But what could this peculiar feature be?

The most obvious candidate, I suppose, is sensitivity. Children do not often have strong vested interests in mathematical problems, scientific hypotheses or German words, so being taught that a solution is incorrect, a hypothesis falsified or a word mistranslated rarely causes them much distress. By contrast, children who subscribe to a moral standard have a conative, affective and behavioural attachment to it, so are quite likely to be affronted by attempts to teach them that their standard is unjustified. At least in educational contexts where the existing moral commitments of children are unknown, it may seem prudent to try to avoid confrontation by favouring nondirective moral inquiry as far as possible.

But the fact that moral inquiry is more likely to trespass on sensitivities than other forms of inquiry is not reason enough for moral educators to step back from the task of transmitting such knowledge as we have. We do children no favours by being coy about the good reasons there are for regarding moral objections to masturbation as unjustified and justificatory appeals to what is natural as unsound. We want children to understand that progress can be made in moral inquiry, and that progress consists as often in the refutation of justificatory arguments as in their vindication. Of course educators should be aware of the possibility that children will have existing attachments to unjustified moral standards, and should take all reasonable steps to minimise the distress caused by exposure to decisive objections to those standards. But they should not play down or soft pedal the objections, nor collude in attempts to avoid their implications.

It is perhaps worth emphasising again that directive teaching need not be didactic. Teaching a child that a moral standard to which she subscribes is unjustified need not, and usually will not, be a matter of instruction or exposition. It can, and usually will, be a matter of ensuring that she encounters, in her reading, viewing or discussions with others, the compelling arguments against her standard, and has opportunities to reflect on those arguments and come to appreciate their force. The aim of persuading her that her standard is unjustified is more likely to be achieved by giving her a nudge in the right direction and space to think than by telling her what to believe and why. The use of nondidactic teaching methods does not innoculate children against the discomfort of having their moral commitments challenged, but it does allow them to manage their discomfort and rethink their commitments at their own pace, and thus reduces the risk of confrontation and entrenchment.

There are, moreover, general reasons for thinking that educators should be as strenuous in their efforts to persuade children of what is known to be true and dissuade them of what is known to be false as they are in their efforts *not* to persuade children of things whose truth value is unknown. To be sure, educators who fall down on the latter job are judged more harshly than those who fall down on the former. Failure to refrain from directive teaching in circumstances of epistemic uncertainty is no doubt more harmful to children than failure to teach directively in circumstances of epistemic certainty. But, notwithstanding the asymmetry of these educational failings, the twin duties of teaching directively what is known and nondirectively what is unknown are equally incumbent on educators. A central aim of education is to bring it about that children form and revise their beliefs rationally, and this requires that they are consistently taught to believe claims confirmed by relevant evidence and argument, to disbelieve claims disconfirmed by relevant evidence and argument, and to suspend judgment or form their own views on claims for which the relevant evidence and argument is ambiguous. Fostering responsible epistemic agency is, at least in part, a matter of modelling and commending appropriate epistemic responses; and the appropriate epistemic response to false propositions, unjustified standards and unsound arguments is to reject them.

Two sites of moral education

Rational moral education, then, involves moral formation, directive moral inquiry and nondirective moral inquiry. Moral educators should cultivate children's subscription to the conflict-averting and cooperation-sustaining standards whose currency in society ameliorates the problem of sociality; they should help children to see that these standards are justified and why, and that some other standards are not justified and why; and they should facilitate open-ended discussion of moral standards and justificatory arguments about which there is reasonable disagreement.

This account of rational moral education is neutral with respect to the question of where children are morally educated and by whom. I take it, however, that the primary sites of moral education are the home and the school, and that the primary moral educators are parents and teachers. So it will perhaps be useful to say something about the division of educational labour between parents and teachers, and about the difficulties that can arise when they have different conceptions of the moral educational task.

Suppose, first, that parents and teachers are equally committed to the sort of rational moral education I have described. They both recognise that moral education must involve moral formation, directive moral inquiry and nondirective moral inquiry, and they broadly agree on which moral standards and justificatory arguments should be taught in which ways. Should they regard themselves as sharing responsibility for the provision of all elements of moral education, or should they divide the work between them, each taking responsibility for the provision of their assigned elements? Might it make sense, for example, to say that parents should take charge of children's moral formation and teachers of engaging them in moral inquiry?

A division of educational labour along these lines is not without appeal. The process of moral formation begins when children are very young, long before they start school. And parents undoubtedly enjoy certain advantages over teachers when it comes to exercising the formative influences that result in subscription to moral standards. The greater intimacy and interdependency of the parent–child relationship means that children are typically, though by no means invariably, more receptive to the prescribing, modelling, rewarding and punishing in which moral formation consists when their parents are doing it than when their teachers are. Correlatively, leading children in inquiry and discussion is the stock-in-trade of teachers, and classrooms are more auspicious environments for the disciplined scrutiny of standards and arguments than kitchens, sitting rooms and bedrooms. Moreover, effective facilitation of moral inquiry requires a secure understanding of its subject matter – of the range of moral standards to which people subscribe and the justificatory arguments advanced in their support, and of the status and soundness of those standards and arguments. Because teachers are trained and accredited and parents are not, it is easier to ensure and safer to assume that teachers adequately understand the subject matter of moral inquiry than that parents do.

At most, however, these considerations show that, in practice, more of the work of moral formation will be done at home than in school and more of the work of moral inquiry will be done in school than at home. They do *not* show that there is reason to favour a principled division of educational responsibilities. To the contrary, things are likely to go much better when parents and teachers are collaboratively engaged in both kinds of educational work, for reasons we have already noted. First, when parents demand that children comply with a moral standard, or punish them for failing to comply with it, they should at least sometimes explain or invite reflection on why the standard is authoritative. It is by no means necessary to follow up every formative intervention with an explanation or invitation of this kind, but nor can parents opt out of moral inquiry altogether, if children's subscription to moral standards is to be appropriately tied to justificatory beliefs. And second, while schools are certainly places of focused inquiry and discussion, they are not only that: they are also sites of cooperation and conflict, coercion and rebellion, kindness and cruelty. They are social contexts in which children's intentions, feelings and habits are unavoidably shaped by their encounters with each other and with those in authority. It does not follow that teachers *must* engage in moral formation, but for them to refrain from doing so would be tantamount to educational negligence. Universally-enlisting and penalty-endorsing subscription to conflict-averting and cooperation-sustaining standards is needed precisely to help human beings navigate the challenges presented by social spaces like schools. Teachers are extraordinarily well placed to cultivate such subscription in children, through the disciplinary and pastoral interventions they must in any case make to ensure that schools are safe, peaceful and conducive to learning. Where parents and teachers share a commitment to rational moral education, then, they should share responsibility for the provision of all its elements.

But now suppose that parents and teachers do not share this commitment. Imagine a child whose teachers are committed to educating her rationally, but whose parents have a rather different conception of their educational role, who see it as their task to inculcate in their child a strict moral code, perhaps a religious one, in such a way as to insulate it from criticism. Assuming that it is not within the power of the teachers in this scenario to change the minds of the parents, and that they are mindful of the trouble caused for children by too much dissonance between home and school, should they draw back to some extent from the requirements of rational moral education? Or should they pursue exactly the same combination of moral formation and directive and nondirective moral inquiry as they would if the child's parents were on the same page?

Certainly teachers should try to be sensitive to the kind of moral education children are receiving at home. Where they know that a child has been taught by her parents to comply with a moral standard without question, they should think carefully about how to introduce the idea that the standard may not be justified, or may be of uncertain justificatory status. They should avoid, where possible, flatly contradicting what parents say or openly criticising their educational practices. Teachers can do much to take the sting out of dissonance between home and school by being respectful of parents and diplomatic in their treatment of moral standards whose justificatory status is misrepresented in the home.

Beyond the demand for sensitivity, respect and diplomacy, however, I do not think the responsibilities of teachers are affected by an absence of parental commitment to rational moral education. First, teachers should still try to cultivate in children subscription to basic moral standards and to persuade them that the problem-of-sociality justification for these standards is sound. Here, the bone of contention with parents trying to inculcate a more comprehensive moral code will not usually be the basic standards themselves – these, after all, are common to more or less all established moral codes – but rather the justification offered for them, or perhaps the idea that the question of justification should be raised at all. Where the difficulty is that parents are teaching a different justification, teachers can reduce conflict by emphasising the point that the problem–of–sociality justification does not exclude justifications of other kinds. Children already wedded to the view that moral standards are authoritative because ordained by God can be helped to see that some of those standards may *also* be authoritative because necessary for the stability of human social groups. Less can be done about the tension between home and school when parents discourage the asking of justificatory questions altogether: in this case the conflict is one children must simply learn how to manage. It is more important to make children aware that they are not obliged to accept any proposition or standard without reason than it is to spare them the discomfort of disagreement between their parents and teachers.

Second, teachers should still teach controversial moral standards and justificatory arguments in such a way as to keep open the question of their status and soundness. Insofar as children have been taught at home that certain moral standards are justified, it may be jarring for them, initially, to find those same standards treated in school as matters of debate. But to teach a standard as controversial is precisely to make clear that at least one argument for subscribing to it is at least plausible, and thus that reasonable people can reasonably believe it to be justified. So nondirective inquiry into controversial standards and arguments need not, and should not, be unduly distressing for the children already attached to them.

And third, teachers should still try to ensure that children recognise unjustified moral standards and unsound justificatory arguments for what they are. It is directive teaching of this kind that is most likely to cause trouble for children whose parents are determined to bring them to the opposite conclusions. Where parents and teachers are advocating diametrically opposed verdicts on moral standards, the pressure on children can be acute. As I have already suggested, this is a pressure that can be somewhat alleviated by the avoidance of didactic teaching methods: it will, usually, be both counterproductive and unkind for teachers to hold forth on the irrationality of standards parents are actively endorsing and enforcing in the home. Better to provide avenues and opportunities for children to come gradually to the realisation that their parents may be in error. But, while this may ease the pressure, it will not eliminate it. As with children who have been discouraged from asking justificatory questions, children who have been taught to endorse unjustified moral standards cannot be shielded from the disorientating effects of educational conflict. Teachers are understandably reluctant to unsettle children by impugning what they have learned at home; but to leave them in thrall to moral standards wholly lacking in rational support would be to do them a far greater disservice.

7

GIVING OFFENCE, GOING PRIVATE AND BEING GAY

Rational moral education requires that moral standards are taught in different ways depending on whether they are justified, unjustified or of uncertain justificatory status. A task of the first importance for moral educators is, therefore, to assign standards to be taught to the correct justificatory categories. Parents and teachers need to know when they should be cultivating full moral commitment, when they should be discouraging it, and when they should be equipping children to form their own considered views.

Let me emphasise that there are three justificatory categories, not two: the task here is *not* to classify moral standards as justified or unjustified in the teeth of reasonable disagreement about them. *That* would be a tall order indeed. The task is rather to distinguish standards about whose justification there is reasonable disagreement from standards about whose justification there is not. This is a tall order too, but not nearly as tall as that of settling all the justificatory disputes in the moral sphere.

To show that this is a task by which we should not be unduly daunted, I should like, in this chapter, to give some examples of moral standards whose justificatory classification may not be immediately obvious and work through the process of establishing it. The standards I shall discuss are these:

1. Do not give offence.
2. Do not privately educate your children.
3. Do not engage in homosexual acts.

Each of these standards is such that some but not all people subscribe to it, and some but not all people believe subscription to be justified. The question, in each case, is whether the disagreement about justification is reasonable. Are there good arguments both for and against subscription to these standards, making it appropriate to teach them nondirectively? Or does the weight of argument fall decisively on one side, licensing efforts to persuade children that subscription is, or is not, justified? I shall consider each standard in turn.

Giving offence

Is it morally objectionable to say or do things that cause offence? It seems clear that, in some contexts at least, the exclamation 'That's offensive!' is intended as a moral reproof. It is designed both to condemn what has been said or done and to identify what is morally objectionable about it. But it seems equally clear that, in these same contexts, at least some people justly convicted of offensive speech or action are inclined to reply 'So what?' The implication of their reply is that they do not see the offensiveness of their conduct as giving them a moral reason to refrain from it. How reasonable is this disagreement?

Let us begin with some clarifications and distinctions. First, the question of whether it is morally wrong to *give* offence needs to be kept apart from questions about whether and when people are justified in *taking* offence. The undue readiness of people to 'consider as an injury to themselves any conduct which they have a distaste for, and resent it as an outrage to their feelings' (Mill, 1989 [1859], p.84) is a longstanding complaint of champions of liberty, and perhaps a warranted one. It is certainly interesting to inquire into the principles by which our offence-taking should be governed. But it is also a distraction from the matter in hand.

Second, it is no objection to the idea that offence-giving is morally wrong to observe that sometimes honesty demands it, or justice cannot be served without it. Moral subscription is not overriding; we are perfectly used to negotiating conflicts between our various moral standards, and between our moral and non-moral standards. The question is not whether giving offence is to be avoided at all costs, but whether it is to be avoided in general and other things being equal.

Nor, third, is it an objection to a moral prohibition on giving offence to insist that people cannot be held responsible for offending others inadvertently, at any rate when the offended sensibilities are not ones they could have been expected to know about. It is plainly true that the absence of an intention to offend is a mitigating factor when assessing culpability for offensive conduct, but that fact has no bearing on the arguments for and against a standard that prohibits it. All standards of conduct are such that failures to comply with them can be more or less deliberate and more or less blameworthy: standards pertaining to offence-giving pose no special challenges in this respect.

Fourth, there is a difference between morality and manners. It does not follow from the fact that offending people is rude or discourteous that it is morally wrong. There is no reason why conduct cannot be simultaneously ill-mannered and immoral, though it is perhaps unusual to worry about considerations of etiquette once considerations of morality are in play. But plenty of conduct qualifies as ill-mannered without coming close to qualifying as immoral. The myriad rules and rituals by which human beings regulate such everyday activities as dining, conversing and transacting can be breached in innumerable ways without incurring anything like the disapprobation reserved for breaches of moral standards. Offence-giving must be more than just impolite if the case for a moral prohibition on it is to be made good.

Fifth, and finally, conduct that is morally objectionable *and* gives offence is not necessarily morally objectionable *because* it gives offence. Oppressive or discriminatory speech, for example, is morally wrong because of the harm it does to those oppressed or discriminated against, and precisely because it is wrong it frequently gives offence. Perhaps we shall want to say that sexist or racist remarks are wrong *both* because of the harm they do to women and people of colour *and* because of the offence they give to decent human beings; but we need not admit the latter in order to affirm the former. There are, moreover, plenty of contexts in which speech of this kind offends no one who hears it (think, for example, of misogynistic jokes told in private among like-minded men), and the absence of offended parties in these contexts hardly makes it less deserving of moral condemnation.

So, in light of these preliminaries, what are the prospects of vindicating the moral standard 'Do not give offence'? With the standard stated in this unqualified way, they are not good. The class of offences people can give to one another is large and heterogeneous and some kinds of offence are implausible candidates for moral regulation. Think of affronts to the senses. We certainly talk of being offended when our senses are affronted by, for example, people with unpleasant body odour, or people playing loud music in our vicinity. But the inconvenience to which we are put by bad smells and loud noises does not seem serious enough to justify the sort of policing and penalising involved in moral regulation. Such annoyances are as likely as any other kind of offence to prompt the exclamation 'That's offensive!' but here the exclamation does not usually carry the weight of a moral reproof.

Joel Feinberg draws a basic distinction between 'offensive nuisances' and 'profound offences' (Feinberg, 1988). Offensive nuisances are affronts to the senses or to 'lower order sensibilities': in these cases the offence given is 'relatively trivial or shallow', tied to 'direct perception of the offending conduct' and 'personal', in the sense that 'the offended party thinks of *himself* as the wronged victim' (ibid., pp.57–58). Profound offences, by contrast, are affronts to 'higher order sensibilities': here the offence given is 'deep, profound, shattering, serious', not tied to direct perception (the offended party need not witness the offending conduct) and 'at least partly impersonal', in the sense that the offended party does not, or does not only, 'feel aggrieved on his own behalf' (ibid., pp.58–59). Affronts to sensibilities differ from affronts to the senses in that they are 'mediated by recognition or belief' (ibid., p.16); and affronts to higher order sensibilities differ from affronts to lower order sensibilities in that they are mediated by the belief that a standard has been violated. The latter distinction is glossed by Feinberg as follows:

> We are disgusted at the sight of a person eating a dripping, wriggling, live sea slug, simply because we recognise it to be such, and given the character of our gastronomic sensibility, that recognition is quite sufficient to induce disgust. It

is not necessary to the process that we hold a moral principle, or even a specific moral conviction, that eating sea slugs is cruel, sinful, or wicked. It is simply disgusting in some pre-rational, nondiscursive way, and that is an end to the matter. An additional step is involved in the production of disgust by offense to higher level sensibilities. When we see a strapping young man arrogantly push aside an aged lady in his haste to occupy the only remaining seat on the bus, we recognize the items in our experience as *young man, aged lady, push,* and *seat,* and that brings to mind a moral principle prescribing the proper conduct of persons of the type perceived. Then, in virtue of the perceived gross violation of that principle, we are disgusted.

(ibid., p.16)

Profound offences, then, are those given to people by words or deeds that violate standards to which they subscribe. Insofar as we are tempted by the thought that people should be morally protected from offence-giving, it is, I think, profound offence-giving we usually have in mind. So, to maximise the plausibility of the moral prohibition under consideration, let us make it a little more specific: is there a sound justification for the moral standard 'do not give profound offence'?

A couple of examples may help to focus our inquiry. In an entertaining catalogue of offences given by people behaving in unpleasant ways on a bus ride, Feinberg includes these two stories of profound offence:

> *Story 11.* A strapping youth enters the bus and takes a seat directly in your line of vision. He is wearing a T-shirt with a cartoon across his chest of Christ on the cross. Underneath the picture appear the words 'Hang in there, baby!'
> *Story 12.* After taking the seat next to you a passenger produces a bundle wrapped in a large American flag. The bundle contains, among other things, his lunch, which he proceeds to eat. Then he spits into the star-spangled corner of the flag and uses it first to clean his mouth and then to blow his nose. Then he uses the main striped part of the flag to shine his shoes.
>
> *(ibid., pp.11–12)*

Assume that the T-shirt-wearer knows his attire will give profound offence to religious passengers, and the flag-defiler knows his actions will profoundly offend patriotic ones. Assume, too, that the T-shirt-wearer – an atheist – is unmoved by religious reasons for action, and the flag-defiler – a cosmopolitan – is unmoved by patriotic ones. And assume, finally, that neither Christians nor American patriots are marginalised, excluded or otherwise disadvantaged groups in the society in which these events take place, so the actions of the T-shirt-wearer and the flag-defiler do not qualify as oppressive or discriminatory. These stories, with these assumptions, will serve as paradigm cases of the conduct targeted by a moral prohibition on profound offence-giving.

What, then, might be said in support of such a prohibition? There are three justificatory arguments with at least prima facie appeal. First, it might be argued that profound offence is sufficiently distressing for the offended party to qualify as a harm. There is a robustly justified moral prohibition on causing harm, so if profoundly offending people counts as harming them, it is straightforwardly morally wrong. On one plausible account of harm, a person is harmed when she suffers a setback to her interests, and it looks as though everyone has an interest in not being deeply distressed. The love and reverence felt by Christians for Christ, and by patriots for their flag, make it painful for them to witness the casual desecrations described in our paradigm cases.

As harms go, the psychological discomfort of profound offence may not compare in severity with physical injury, loss of freedom or social exclusion, but the argument does not depend on the harm being severe. Severe and mild harms alike are ruled out by the prohibition on harmful conduct. Our ability to grade harms by their severity matters a great deal when it comes to choice situations in which doing harm is unavoidable, or a harmful course of action must be weighed against, say, a dishonest one. If we must sometimes choose the lesser of two evils, we need some way of quantifying the evils in question. But in most situations, when we are not presented with dilemmas of this kind, to recognise something as a harm is to have a clear moral reason not to do it.

Second, it might be argued that, even if profound offence is not itself a harm, it directly contributes to one. Perhaps, for example, the cumulative effect of repeated affronts to one's higher order sensibilities is a loss of self-respect. John Weckert puts the point like this:

> When someone makes a remark or exhibits conduct that we find offensive, we may feel that we are not being respected as persons in the way that we ought to be. Our self-respect may be lessened to some extent. Too much of this conduct may cause us to see ourselves as people of little worth.
>
> (Weckert, 2007, p.29)

The thought here is that regular exposure to profound offence takes a heavy psychological toll. Shocks to higher order sensibilities may not be intrinsically harmful, but the challenge they present to our values and loyalties is burdensome, and as the shocks multiply the burden becomes greater. Eventually, under the yoke of repeated affronts to the things we hold dear, we begin to lose our self-respect – and *that* is an unambiguous harm.

And third, it might be argued that profoundly offending people is wrong because it undermines the stability of human social groups: it results in outbreaks of conflict and breakdowns in cooperation. Offensive conduct can cause trouble of this kind even if it does not harm, either directly or indirectly, the offended parties. The problem is simply that people are antagonised by and disinclined to cooperate with those who profoundly offend them.

In Chapter Five we noted the roles played by 'competition' and 'diffidence' in making 'the naturall condition of mankind' a state of war in which 'every man is enemy to every man' (Hobbes, 1929 [1651], p.96). But, alongside these two 'causes of quarrell' in the state of nature, Hobbes identifies a third, which he labels 'glory'. We are led into conflict with one another not only by competition for scarce resources and distrust of our competitors, but also by threats to our reputation or self-esteem:

> For every man looketh that his companion should value him, at the same rate he sets upon himselfe: And, upon all signes of contempt, or undervaluing, naturally endeavours, as far as he dares (which amongst them that have no common power to keep them in quiet, is far enough to make them destroy each other,) to extort a greater value from his contemners, by dommage; and from others, by the example.
>
> *(ibid., pp.95–96.)*

Glory or reputation is so important to people, Hobbes thinks, that they can be driven to violence by words and deeds that appear to undervalue them 'either direct in their Persons, or by reflexion in their Kindred, their Friends, their Nation, their Profession, or their Name' (ibid., p.96). It is no stretch to suggest that the kinds of offensive conduct with which we are presently concerned appear to the offended parties to undervalue them in just these ways. So, to avoid the violence consequent on 'signes of contempt', a moral prohibition on profound offence-giving may be necessary.

We can imagine rather easily the reaction of a gung-ho American patriot to the behaviour of the flag-defiler in Story 12. He would not be, nor perceive himself to be, harmed by the desecration of the flag; but he would feel deeply insulted by it, defensive of his country and his compatriots, and warranted in making a robust response – perhaps a violent one. And if it turned out that defiler and patriot were en route to the same meeting, the prospects of their working together cooperatively to bring the meeting to a satisfactory conclusion would be significantly reduced by their encounter on the bus.

Each of these arguments has something to be said for it. It is not unreasonable to suppose that profoundly offending people does them a kind of harm, or contributes to a kind of harm, or creates avoidable conflict between offender and offended, and to conclude on these grounds that profound offence-giving is morally wrong. But there are also things to be said *against* the three arguments that make it difficult to see them as either individually or collectively decisive.

With regard to the claim that profound offence is a species of harm, it must be admitted that 'harm' is a tricky term to pin down – as is 'interests', if it is agreed that a person is harmed when she suffers a setback to her interests. It may be true, in one sense, that everyone has an interest in not being distressed, where this is just another way of saying that no one wants to be distressed; but there are plenty of contexts in which we distinguish the things people have an interest in from the things they merely want. My present desire for a large gin and tonic does not imply that I have an interest in having one, or that my being prevented from having one (by the rules of the library in which I'm working) is a harm to me. Feinberg proposes that interests proper are of two kinds: *welfare interests*, which are those all human beings share, in such goods as health, safety, sustenance, shelter, company and liberty; and *ultimate interests*, which are those we have in the fulfilment of our 'relatively deep-rooted and stable wants', whatever they might be (Feinberg, 1987, p.45). It is only setbacks to our welfare and ultimate interests that ought to be classified as harms.

On this proposal there is a whole gamut of unpleasant experiences, sensations and emotions, including the ones associated with being profoundly offended, that do not count as harms. Feinberg writes:

> Not everything that we dislike or resent, and wish to avoid, is harmful to us. Eating a poorly cooked dish may be unpleasant, but if the food is unspoiled, the experience is not likely to be harmful. So it is with a large variety of other experiences, from watching a badly performed play to receiving a rude comment. These experiences can distress, offend, or irritate us, without harming any of our interests. They come to us, are suffered for a time, and then go, leaving us as whole and undamaged as we were before.
>
> *(ibid., p.45)*

What of the claim that repeated exposure to profound offence undermines the self-respect of the offended? The difficulty here is that the connection between being profoundly offended and suffering a loss of self-respect may not be tight enough to warrant a moral prohibition on offence-giving. We can certainly imagine cases in which a person is so frequently and grievously offended by those around her that she comes to see herself as having little worth, but cases of this kind may not be all that common. It is hard to see how either the T-shirt-wearer or the flag-defiler in our paradigm cases could fairly be accused of damaging the self-esteem of his fellow passengers. In these cases, and in many others, there is no targeting of specific individuals and no protracted campaign of offences whose cumulative effect might be to erode the confidence of the offended.

Moreover, there are at least some cases of profound offence that contribute to an overall *benefit* to the offended party. Think of shocks to higher order sensibilities that bring home to people the irrationality of their subscription to a violated standard, and thus help them to begin the process of unsubscribing. Suppose we replace the T-shirt in Story 11 with one displaying a smiley face and the slogan 'Smile if you masturbate'. Passengers raised to believe that masturbation is wicked may be profoundly offended by this T-shirt; but they may also be prompted by the force of their reaction to reflect on the grounds for their belief, and this may be the first step on the road to relinquishing it. Given that one familiar motive for publicly violating other people's standards is precisely to make them consider the possibility that their standards are unjustified, and given that some of the standards people subscribe to really *are* unjustified, it would be hasty to assume that cases of beneficial offence-giving are exceptional.

If many profound offences form no part of a cumulatively damaging pattern, and some result in a benefit to the offended, the contention that they normally or characteristically result in a harm looks shaky.

Finally, as regards the claim that profound offence poses a threat to social stability, it must be asked whether a moral prohibition on offence-giving is the best way to tackle the problem. It is one possibility, to be sure, but not the only one. Another is to treat profound offence as one of the troublesome features of life in human social groups that morality helps us to cope with. On this view, people will sometimes offend each other, just as they will sometimes compete, clash or disagree with each other, and what we need from a moral code are ways of managing these hazards. We subscribe to conflict-averting and cooperation-sustaining standards not to rid the world of competition, disagreement and offence, but to contain them, to ensure that they do not escalate into violence or undermine our joint ventures. It is injurious reactions to offence-giving that must be morally prohibited, not offence-giving itself.

Still, it might be replied, why not a prohibition on both? If people undertook *neither* to react violently to offence *nor* to give offence, the threat of offence-related conflict would presumably be reduced still further. Should we not take a belt and braces approach to the problem? An obvious answer is that, while the problem of sociality must be solved, we should favour the solution that places the fewest constraints on liberty. If we can keep the peace by prohibiting violent reactions to offence, we ought not to prohibit offence-giving too – especially if we think that the freedom to act in ways that violate other people's standards may be necessary for social progress. Mill famously contends that people must be at liberty to break with tradition and custom if they are 'to commence new practices, and set the example of more enlightened conduct, and better taste and sense in human life' (Mill, 1989 [1859], p.64). On this view, for as long as questions about the right, best or happiest way to live remain unsettled, we should endorse social arrangements that allow people to experiment with a wide range of lifestyles and practices, including those by which others are profoundly offended:

> That mankind are not infallible; that their truths, for the most part, are only half-truths; that unity of opinion, unless resulting from the fullest and freest comparison of opposite opinions, is not desirable, and diversity not an evil, but a good, until mankind are much more capable than at present of recognizing all sides of the truth, are principles applicable to men's modes of action, not less than to their opinions. As it is useful that while mankind are imperfect there should be different opinions, so is it that there should be different experiments of living; that free scope should be given to varieties of character, short of injury to others; and that the worth of different modes of life should be proved practically, when any one thinks fit to try them.
>
> *(ibid., p.57)*

So there are powerful objections to each of the three plausible arguments for a moral prohibition on offence-giving. People who knowingly give profound offence can certainly be convicted of bad manners, and manners are not unimportant; but whether they can also be convicted of immorality is an open question. There is room for reasonable disagreement among reasonable people about the justificatory status of the standard 'do not give profound offence'; and for that reason the standard should be taught nondirectively by moral educators.

Going private

Another moral standard on which opinion is divided is 'do not privately educate your children'. At least in left-leaning social circles, it is common for parents to refuse to consider the option of private education, to feel guilty if they do consider it, and to be censured by friends and colleagues if they take it up. For other parents, though, private education is simply one option among others, to be weighed up in light of the numerous practical considerations that bear on school choice, but certainly not to be ruled out on principle. So is there or is there not a justified moral prohibition on going private?

Again, it will be well to start with some clarifications. First, moral objections to private education tend to assume a society in which (i) an adequate state education is freely available to all, (ii) the fees charged by private schools significantly exceed the per capita funding for children in state schools and (iii) only a minority of parents can afford to pay those fees. Many contemporary societies are roughly like this, so I will make these assumptions too. But it is worth bearing in mind that the morality of going private looks a little different when the education provided by state schools is patently inadequate, when private school fees are lower than or commensurate with per capita funding in state schools, or when all parents can afford to pay those fees.

Second, the question of whether it is morally wrong to go private must be distinguished from the question of whether the state ought to abolish private schools (or to constrain them in ways that significantly reduce their capacity to confer unfair advantage, for example by capping their fees at the level of per capita funding in state schools). Perhaps the state *should* abolish or significantly constrain private schools, but if it were to do so there would be no need to worry about the morality of going private. The moral question before us arises precisely because expensive, advantage-conferring private education is legally permitted and readily available. Nor should it be assumed that someone who favours a moral prohibition on going private must also favour the abolition of private schools: I might take the view that, in a liberal society, the state should not use its coercive power to prevent citizens from purchasing private education for their children, even though this is something they have good moral reason not to do.

Third, and relatedly, the claim that it is wrong to go private is different from the claim that it is wrong *for people who favour the abolition of private schools* to go private. In the UK at least, decisions by politicians on the left to send their children to private schools attract much disapprobation in the media, but not on the grounds that going private is objectionable per se. The reason for the outcry is that there is thought to be a contradiction between asserting that private schools should be abolished and availing oneself of their services: to contradict oneself in this way, it is alleged, is to be guilty of hypocrisy. Whether that charge sticks need not detain us here, though it is worth pointing out that the supposed contradiction is not easy to pin down. On the face of it, it is perfectly consistent to hold that everyone would be better off if some practice were legally prohibited, but to continue engaging in that practice for as long as it is legally permitted. In any case, our present concern is not with the vice of hypocrisy, but with the possibility that it is morally wrong for everyone, regardless of their political views, to privately educate their children.

What, then, might be said in support of this possibility? Why might it be wrong for parents to purchase for their children a better-than-usual education that enhances their prospects of success in the labour market? Advocates of a moral prohibition on going private have only one answer to this question, but it is a powerful one: parents who privately educate their children unfairly advantage them over children who are not privately educated. If it is granted that there is a basic moral requirement to treat others fairly, and if it is true that parents who send their children to private schools are treating children in state schools unfairly, the case for a moral prohibition looks strong.

To see how the lavishing of resources on one child's education can be unfair on another, we need to recognise that the value of education in people's lives is at least partly *positional*. The goods acquired by learning (knowledge, understanding, habits, competences, commitments, etc.) may have great intrinsic value to those who acquire them, but they also have instrumental value as means to further ends – in particular, the end of securing and retaining a rewarding and well-paid job. In a competitive labour market with only a limited number of rewarding and well-paid jobs available, the instrumental value of educational goods is positional: the value of my learning depends on whether I have learned more or less than my competitors. Adam Swift explains the idea, and its implications for private education, as follows:

> education is, in part, a positional good. As an instrumental means to jobs and the money that goes with them, what matters is not how much education one has, or how good it is, but how much one has, or how good it is, relative to the others with whom one is competing for jobs. This gives education something of a zero-sum aspect: the better educated you are, the worse for me (and vice versa). While there is some controversy about whether private schools are in fact better, all things considered, for the children who go to them, than state schools would be ... it seems undeniable that, in terms of competition in the labour market, at least some private schools do indeed bestow considerable advantages on the children who attend them. But, because of the zero-sum aspect, this means that such schools inevitably make things worse for those who do not go to them.
>
> *(Swift, 2004, p.11)*

By choosing to privately educate my children, then, I am 'unfairly buying them a higher place in the queue for well-rewarded and interesting jobs' (ibid., p.14). And this does seem unfair on the children who are thereby moved further down the queue than they would otherwise be.

In the background of this argument against going private are some assumptions about what *should* determine success in the labour market. Roughly, the people at the front of the queue should be the ones who *deserve* to be there, and what people deserve is a function of what they can be held responsible for. A person can be held responsible for doing better at school than her peers if her better performance is attributable to her greater talent and hard work; but she cannot be held responsible if it is attributable to her parents' financial investment in her education. As Harry Brighouse puts it: 'Where someone's level of success in the labour market is due *to some extent* to their family's background circumstances, or their family's choices, it is unreasonable to hold the competitor responsible for that level of success *to that extent*' (Brighouse, 2000, p.117). Fairness in a competitive labour market requires not only that the best jobs go to the best qualified candidates, but that candidates' qualifications are determined by their talent and effort, not by the cost of their education. One advantage of a state education system is that it helps to ensure approximate equality of educational provision across the system; but that advantage is disastrously compromised if a wealthy few opt out of the system and educate their children privately.

So runs the argument for the standard 'do not privately educate your children'. The argument is weighty, but it is also vulnerable to some telling objections. One worry is that it seems to rule out a lot more than going private: parents determined not to give their children an unfair advantage over others would have to stop doing all sorts of things that we ordinarily regard as morally permissible. A much discussed example in the literature is the practice of reading bedtime stories:

> Some children are read bedtime stories by their parents, others are not so lucky. Those who get stories will tend to have better lives than those who do not, partly because those who have had stories tend to be better placed in the competition for jobs and their attendant rewards. The mechanisms by which advantaged parents convey advantage to their children are many and myriad and they remain so even if we focus exclusively on *competitive* advantage: the kind of advantage that makes things worse for those who do not have it.
>
> *(Swift, 2004, p.13)*

Parents who read their children bedtime stories, or engage them in lively conversation over the dinner table, or take them to museums and galleries, advantage them over children whose parents are unable or unwilling to do these things. The advantage appears to be unfair in just the same way as the advantage conferred by private education: children are moved up the queue for desirable jobs on the basis of educational progress for which they cannot be held responsible. And yet it seems unthinkable to suggest that *these* things should be morally prohibited. So why should parents who opt for private education be picked out for moral censure?

Criteria for distinguishing acceptable from unacceptable ways of conferring advantage on one's children have been suggested. Brighouse and Swift propose that advantage-conferring is permissible if it is a by-product of activities that are part and parcel of intimate familial relationships: 'Parents have the right to engage in those activities and interactions with their children that facilitate the realization of the extremely valuable goods that justify the family in the first place' (Brighouse and Swift, 2014, p.118). Reading bedtime stories to children is integral to family life; educating them privately is not. But this criterion is controversial: what justifies the family, if indeed justification is required, is an open question. It is also vague: how we are to delimit the class of activities that are integral to family life is by no means clear. Presumably activities in which parents and children participate together are permissible, but what about activities – clubs, bands, summer camps, Sunday schools – that parents organise for their children but do not participate in? Is there a relevant difference between paying for a weekly piano lesson and paying for a private school?

There are worries, too, about the attempt to distinguish ways in which people can be said to deserve the success attendant on their educational attainment from ways in which they cannot. It is hard to see why those who have the good fortune to be more talented (intelligent, capable, astute) than their peers thereby deserve the goods to which their talents give them access. It makes no difference whether we think of talents as products of nature or nurture: either way, they are not attributes for which their possessors can reasonably be held responsible. It is initially more plausible to suggest that people deserve the goods to which their effort or hard work gives them access, but even here things look less straightforward when it is remembered that the people in question are children. Some children start school with a set of dispositions conducive to serious thought and focused study and others start without those dispositions; of the children in the latter group, some soon pick up the habit of hard work from their teachers and classmates and others are frustratingly resistant to it. The differences between these groups of children are educationally important, but there is little temptation to describe one group as more deserving than another. Plainly there are complex social and psychological stories to be told here: of the many factors that explain why some children are more industrious than others, few lay responsibility for the difference at the door of the children themselves. It looks as though educational success always depends heavily on genetic and environmental luck, to an extent that makes the distinction between deserved and undeserved educational success difficult to maintain. But if that's right, it cannot be an objection to private schools that the success of those who attend them is partially undeserved.

And finally, there are questions to be asked about the scope of the moral requirement to treat others fairly – in particular, about what counts as 'treating others' at all. On the face of it, when a parent chooses to send her child to one school rather than another, she is acting on her child alone, or perhaps on her child and those who attend or work at the school she chooses. It is rather a stretch to say that she is acting on all children, and in a way that might qualify as treating most of them unfairly. Typically, when someone acts to benefit a loved one, we do not regard her as acting on everyone else too, or condemn her for denying them the benefit the loved one has received. The standard 'treat others fairly' is not usually construed as requiring subscribers to refrain from conferring a benefit on anyone unless they plan to confer it on everyone.

Opponents of going private will reply that it is the positionality of educational goods that makes the fair treatment standard applicable to school choice. If I give a colleague a lift to work, I do not leave anyone worse off than they would otherwise have been with respect to making their morning commutes. Getting to work does not have the character of a competition and giving my colleague a lift does not tilt the playing field against her competitors. Getting educated, on the other hand, does have the character of a competition and going private significantly tilts the playing field: that is why school choice falls within the scope of the fairness requirement. The difficulty with this reply is that the positional conception of educational goods may not capture what is actually most important in school choice (and certainly does not capture what many parents *think* is most important). Arguably, at least, it is the intrinsic value of the goods of learning, not their instrumental value as a means of securing employment, that should rightfully govern parents' decisions about where their children go to school. And because the intrinsic value of educational goods is not positional, this way of framing school choice would move it back outside the scope of the fairness requirement.

The argument for the standard 'do not privately educate your children' is not decisively defeated by these objections, but they are strong enough to cast reasonable doubt on it. Like the prohibition on giving offence, the prohibition on going private is neither demonstrably justified nor demonstrably unjustified, and moral educators should therefore teach it nondirectively.

Being gay

The third and final standard I should like to consider is 'do not engage in homosexual acts'. Clearly there are people who subscribe to this moral standard and people who do not. The former stand ready to condemn participants in homosexual acts and, if they experience same-sex attraction themselves, strive to refrain from acting on it and feel guilty if they do act on it; the latter see no reason either to condemn participants in homosexual acts or to refrain from acting on same-sex attraction. What is there to be said for and against this moral prohibition?

Note that the prohibition in question is on homosexual acts, not on homosexual desires or preferences. It is quite possible to endorse a prohibition on homosexual acts without feeling any inclination to condemn people for experiencing same-sex attraction. Whether or not those who object to homosexual acts also object to same-sex attraction depends, presumably, on the degree to which they think the latter is a matter of choice, something over which control can be exercised. The more implausible one finds it to suppose that same-sex attraction is chosen, the less intelligible it is to endorse a prohibition on it. At any rate, it is only the view that people should refrain from acting on same-sex attraction with which we are presently concerned.

There are three notable arguments for the wrongness of homosexual acts. The first, and most familiar, is the argument from scriptural authority. According to some religious believers, what justifies a prohibition on homosexual acts is its authorisation in a sacred text. Conservative Christians, for example, are wont to defend their objection to homosexuality with reference to the following biblical passages:

> You shall not lie with a male as with a woman; it is an abomination.
>
> *(Leviticus 18:22)*

> If a man lies with a man as with a woman, both of them have committed an abomination; they shall be put to death, their blood is upon them.
>
> *(Leviticus 20:13)*

> Therefore God gave them up in the lusts of their hearts to impurity, to the dishonouring of their bodies among themselves, because they exchanged the truth about God for a lie ... Their women exchanged natural relations for unnatural, and the men likewise gave up natural relations with women and were consumed with passion for one another, men committing shameless acts with men and receiving in their own persons the due penalty for their error.
>
> *(Romans 1:24–27)*

These passages are fairly unambiguous. If there are grounds for thinking that biblical injunctions are morally authoritative, the conclusion that homosexual acts are wrong is difficult to avoid.

Second is the so-called 'perverted faculty' argument, according to which we should not put our organs or body-parts to uses that frustrate or disregard their biological functions. Since the biological function of our sexual organs is reproduction, all non-reproductive uses of those organs are ruled out. And the use of the sexual organs in homosexual acts is clearly non-reproductive.

The third argument is a little more complex. Advanced by such natural law theorists as Germain Grisez (1993), John Finnis (1994) and Robert George (1999), the argument infers the impermissibility of homosexual acts from their incompatibility with the realisation of basic human goods. To see how this argument works, it is necessary to understand the moral theory on which it rests.

At the heart of contemporary natural law theory is a distinctive conception of practical reason. On one familiar view, practical reason has no content of its own but consists in working out the most efficient means to the satisfaction of desires. Reason, as Hume puts it, 'is and ought only to be the slave of the passions, and can never pretend to any other office than to serve and obey them' (Hume, 1896 [1739], p.415). Against this view, natural law theorists propose that practical reason supplies us with ends as well as means. The ends built into the structure of practical reason are described as basic human goods, and it is these ends, rather than whatever desires we happen to have, that give us reasons to act. From the fact that I have a *desire* for a particular state of affairs it does not follow that I have a *reason* for trying to bring it about: on the contrary, to be governed by the vicissitudes of desire is precisely *not* to be governed by reason. Rational actions are those that tend to realise basic human goods, whether we are fortunate enough to desire those goods or not.

How are basic human goods to be identified? The suggestion is that we can pick them out them by the *self-evidence* or *intrinsic intelligibility* of the reasons for action they supply. While many of the reasons people give for their actions are intelligible only derivatively, in the sense of being mere links in an explanatory chain, others are intelligible in themselves and thus constitute explanatory endpoints. To illustrate this idea, George tells the story of a graduate student named Adam who, despite having a busy and fulfilling schedule of research and teaching, takes a job covering the night shift in a fast food restaurant (George, 1999, pp.45–48). On being asked why he has done this, Adam replies that he is trying to earn some extra money. This answer, argues George, might be the first part of an explanation, but it can hardly be the whole story. If Adam were to stop here and insist that he wants the extra money just for its own sake, his action would be unintelligible. Adam now goes on to say that he wants the extra money in order to purchase some expensive medicine. Again, though we may be a little further down the road of explanation, we are not there yet, for medicine is no more intrinsically desirable than money. Finally Adam reveals that he needs the medicine for his seriously ill sister. At this point, claims George, we feel no temptation to press Adam further: his explanation is complete. Health, unlike money or medicine, is a basic human good and the want of it is a self-evident or intrinsically intelligible reason for action. Identifying basic human goods, then, is a matter of reflecting on our explanations for action and noting the self-evident reasons that bring them to a close.

The basic human goods identified by this procedure are listed by George as 'life and health, knowledge and aesthetic appreciation, excellence in work and play, and various forms of harmony within each person and among persons (and their communities) and between persons (and their communities) and any wider reaches of reality' (ibid., p.231). To act for the sake of any one of these goods is to act rationally; to act from any other motive is to confound practical reason.

Having identified the ends embedded in practical reason, the next task for natural law theorists is to explain how we are to decide which end to pursue on any given occasion. Given that there are multiple basic human goods and we cannot realise all of them at once, what are the criteria of rational choice between them? The fundamental criterion, argues George, is that we should 'choose and otherwise will those and only those possibilities whose willing is compatible with integral human fulfillment', where integral human fulfillment is not 'a supreme good above or apart from the basic goods', but an ideal of well-being in which the various basic goods are held in balance (ibid., p.51). This fundamental criterion gives rise to a number of 'general norms' or 'modes of responsibility', the most important of which is a prohibition on actions that damage one basic good in the pursuit of another. Choosing 'with a will that another good be sacrificed or damaged' works against the ideal of integral human fulfillment and is therefore 'the mark of immorality' (ibid., p.54).

We are now in a position to follow the logic of the argument for the impermissibility of homosexual acts. Such acts are held to be incompatible with the realisation of basic human goods in two senses: first, there is no basic human good that homosexual acts realise or serve; and second, there is at least one basic human good – harmony within the person – that homosexual acts damage or frustrate.

The only sexual acts capable of realising or serving a basic human good are 'marital' ones – that is, acts of heterosexual intercourse in the context of marriage. Marital acts realise the biological aspect of marital union, and marital union is a basic form of harmony among persons. Heterosexual intercourse unites husband and wife by joining them together in a single reproductive entity: 'coitus is a unitary action in which the male and the female become literally one organism' (ibid., p.168). No other sexual acts, including homosexual ones, can serve this good.

Moreover, homosexual acts actively damage the basic human good of harmony within the person, or personal integration. George explains the idea of personal integration as follows:

> The integration of the various aspects of the self in action or in self-awareness is a basic human good, an intrinsic aspect of fulfillment, the lack of which is a privation. The integration consists, partly, in an awareness and appreciation (which may, of course, be quite informal) of the ontological unity of the different aspects of the self. Also, the inner harmony certainly includes a love of self and a certain degree of self-esteem.
>
> *(ibid., p.166)*

Non-marital sexual acts undermine personal integration because we are motivated to enagage in them by a desire to experience certain sensations and feelings (most obviously, sensations of sexual arousal and release and feelings of closeness or intimacy). When we act on such desires we *use* or *instrumentalise* our bodies to gratify our conscious or experiencing selves. We press our bodies into the service of our minds and thus 'dis-integrate' ourselves. In having sex for the sake of pleasurable sensations and feelings 'one treats the body as a mere extrinsic means: one regards the body as something outside or apart from the subject, and so as a mere object' (ibid., p.164). Things are no better if our motivating desire is not so much to *have* pleasurable experiences as to *give* them to another, for here we are guilty of instrumentalising the bodies of our partners in seeking to gratify their conscious selves. Whether our motive is the giving or the receiving of desired sensations and feelings, we cannot escape the charge of dis-integrating persons and thus violating a basic human good.

These, then, are the arguments for the immorality of homosexual acts. There are serious objections to all three of them. Moreover, unlike the objections to the arguments for prohibitions on giving offence and going private, which show only that there is room for reasonable disagreement on these matters, the objections to the arguments for a prohibition on homosexual acts are decisive: they straightforwardly defeat the arguments in question.

The scriptural authority argument rests on the major premise that the injunctions recorded in a specified sacred text are morally authoritative. But there is no sacred text for which this premise is remotely plausible. One way to show this is by means of *reductio ad absurdum*. We cannot infer that homosexual acts are wrong from the existence of biblical injunctions to refrain from them because that would commit us to similar inferences about the many other forms of conduct prescribed and prohibited in the Bible. Some of those inferences would be patently absurd. The Bible prescribes animal sacrifice (Leviticus 1:5), the execution of witches (Exodus 22.18), the stoning of non-virgin brides (Deuteronomy 22:20–21) and the submission of wives to their husbands (Ephesians 5:22–24). It prohibits eating shellfish (Leviticus 11:10), getting tattoos (Leviticus 19:28), working on the sabbath (Exodus 35:2) and wearing garments made of two kinds of cloth (Leviticus 19:19). Insistence on the moral authority of biblical injunctions comes at a preposterously high price.

Another way to refute the faulty major premise is to consider the beliefs that lie behind it. To hold that biblical prescription justifies moral subscription one must believe (i) that God is a legitimate moral authority by virtue of his omniscience and benevolence and (ii) that the authors of biblical texts were passive conduits for the voice of God, as opposed to active story-tellers, law-makers and theologians shaped by the presuppositions and prejudices of the ancient Hebrew and Greek worlds. Whatever view one takes on the first of these beliefs, the second is decisively refuted by the wealth of biblical criticism and scholarship that shows the books of the Bible to be documents of their time. The Bible cannot but be seen as a human composition, rooted in and responsive to particular historical contexts and shot through with moral and political assumptions that we do not share and cannot justify. This does not rule out the possibility that it records the prophecies and testimonies that preceded and followed the appearance of God in human history, and is for this reason a text of unique importance. But it *does* exclude the possibility of supposing moral standards to be justified simply by the existence of corresponding biblical injunctions.

Similar considerations can be advanced to show the error of attempts to read off the content of morality from any of the sacred texts venerated by faith communities. Citing passages in the Qur'an, the Talmud, the Adi Granth, the Vedas or the Tripitaka to justify moral standards is no more rationally credible than citing passages in the Bible.

The perverted faculty argument also rests on an indefensible major premise. While it may be true that the biological function of the sexual organs is disregarded in homosexual acts, there is simply no reason to hold that functional objects can only be used in accordance with their functions. Consider first such manufactured functional objects as chairs and tables, books and computers, shoes and umbrellas. When I sit on a table or press flowers between the pages of a book, I am certainly using these objects in ways that disregard their functions; but what grounds could there be for a moral prohibition on these extra-functional uses? The same applies to such natural functional objects as human organs and body-parts. Hands have a range of biological functions that includes picking up, holding and manipulating things; feet a range that includes standing, walking and running. If I walk on my hands or pick things up with my feet, I am disregarding these functions, but I am hardly doing something to which a moral objection could be raised. So the wrongness of homosexual acts cannot be inferred merely from the fact that they involve extra-functional uses of the reproductive organs.

Thomas Aquinas recognises the difficulty of prohibiting all extra-functional uses of body-parts and tries to save the perverted faculty argument with reference to the loss of viable reproductive material:

> Nor, in fact, should it be deemed a slight sin for a man to arrange for the emission of semen apart from the proper purpose of generating and bringing up children, on the argument that it is either a slight sin, or none at all, for a person to use a part of the body for a different use than that to which it is directed by nature (say, for instance, one chose to walk on his hands, or to use his feet for something usually done with the hands) because man's good is not much opposed by such inordinate use. However, the inordinate emission of semen is incompatible with the natural good; namely, the preservation of the species.
>
> (Aquinas, Summa Contra Gentiles, Book III, Chapter 122)

Extra-functional uses of the penis, unlike extra-functional uses of the hands and feet, typically result in the emission of semen. This wastage of reproductive material is inimical to the preservation of the species, and that is what justifies a moral prohibition on male homosexual and masturbatory acts and contracepted heterosexual acts. (Interestingly, female homosexual and masturbatory acts are untouched by this line of reasoning, because they do not result in a loss of reproductive material.)

This amended version of the argument might carry some weight if semen were a commodity in short supply. If there were some danger of non-reproductive uses of the penis leaving human beings with insufficient semen to propagate the species, we should perhaps have reason to desist from such uses. There is, however, no such danger. Semen is an abundant resource and individual supplies are rapidly replenished after each emission. So the perverted faculty argument cannot be rescued by connecting disregard for the reproductive function of sexual organs with the wastage of reproductive material.

Finally, the basic human goods argument is incoherent even within the terms of the natural law theory it assumes. Let us allow, for the sake of argument, that practical reason has the features natural law theorists ascribe to it: it supplies us with ends as well as means, and the ends are identifiable by their intrinsic intelligibility. Let us allow, too, that there is at least a moral question mark over actions that fail to realise or serve a basic human good and actions that damage or frustrate one.

Making these allowances brings us no closer at all to a justified moral objection to homosexuality.

The claim that homosexual acts fail to realise or serve a basic human good is untenable for two reasons. The first is that such acts plainly enhance the intimacy of same-sex relationships, and same-sex relationships obviously qualify as a form of harmony among persons. Natural law theorists argue that heterosexual marriage is the only form of harmony among persons that can be served by sex because heterosexual intercourse is the only sexual act that is biologically unitive. But this puts an arbitrary biological restriction on the ways in which sexual acts can be unifying. In the context of intimate relationships, sex serves to express and celebrate love, to break down emotional barriers, to induce feelings of warmth and tenderness, and to connect and communicate on a deep level. In these respects homosexual and heterosexual acts are equally conducive to harmony among persons. This is a point made by Martha Nussbaum in a response to Finnis:

> [Finnis] assumes without argument that the only sort of community a sexual relationship can create is a 'procreative community'. This is, of course, plainly false. A sexual relationship may create, quite apart from the possibility of procreation, a community of love and friendship, which no religious tradition would deny to be important human goods.
>
> (Finnis and Nussbaum, 1993, p.13)

The second reason for the untenability of the claim that homosexual acts fail to serve a basic human good is that there is a striking omission from the natural law theorists' list of goods. Recall that the list is compiled by asking which reasons for action are intrinsically intelligible, or constitute endpoints of explanation. It can hardly be denied that one familiar endpoint for explanations of human action is pleasure: sometimes our reason for doing things is simply that we enjoy them. Suppose that Adam, the graduate student in George's illustrative story, had offered a different reason for taking the job in the fast food restaurant. Suppose he took the job not because he needs to raise money for medicine for his ill sister, but just because he enjoys working in fast food restaurants. Perhaps it gives him pleasure to focus on relatively simple, manual tasks after spending his days wrestling with impenetrable books and intractable theoretical problems in the library. Or perhaps the restaurant is busy at night and Adam enjoys the heat, energy and banter of the short-order kitchen. Exactly what it is that he likes about the job is unimportant: the point is that, once we know Adam is there because he enjoys it, his decision has been fully explained. That an activity is pleasurable is a self-evident or intrinsically intelligible reason for engaging in it.

But if pleasure qualifies as a basic human good, it is manifestly untrue that no good is realised by homosexual acts. The fact that some people find homosexual acts immensely pleasurable gives them an immediate, intrinsically intelligible reason to engage in them.

What of the claim that homosexual acts damage or frustrate a basic human good – specifically, the good of personal integration? The problem here is that the distinction between actions that instrumentalise the body and actions that respect the ontological unity of the self is deeply obscure; and, insofar as sense can be made of it, it looks as though a large number of ordinary and unobjectionable activities will fall into the former category. Non-marital sexual acts are wrong, it is argued, because they are oriented towards such mental phenomena as sensations of arousal and feelings of intimacy, and the body is used as an extrinsic means of securing these ends. Well, we can choose to talk in that way, but if we describe sensations and feelings as mental phenomena, we are surely obliged to place cognitive apprehensions and aesthetic responses in the same category. If having sex with a view to experiencing pleasure instrumentalises the body, so too does reading books with a view to acquiring knowledge and visiting art galleries with a view to being moved or inspired. Alternatively we can reject the classification of sensations, feelings, apprehensions and responses as mental phenomena and insist that these things are properly predicated of persons, not minds. But if we make this move it can no longer be claimed that non-marital sexual acts instrumentalise the body in pursuit of 'an effect in consciousness' (George, 1999, p.179), for sexual pleasure is now recognised to be an experience of persons as psychosomatic unities.

Michael Perry (1995) and Stephen Macedo (1995) point out that the dis-integrating objection to having sex for pleasure appears to entail the view that it is also wrong to eat for pleasure. George replies, somewhat unpersuasively, that people very rarely eat for the sake of pleasure alone: most of the time 'the pleasure of eating is integrated into people's larger worthwhile projects' (George, 1999, p.150). He agrees, however, that if people did eat purely for pleasure, their actions would be morally objectionable:

> a person could, we imagine, pursue pleasure in eating or chewing gum in a way divorced from larger projects such that his activity could only accurately be described as 'pleasuring himself' in a way analogous to the masturbator or the psychedelic drug-tripper … In that case we would say that eating and chewing gum damage personal integrity insofar as those acts effect an existential alienation of the body from the conscious self.
>
> *(ibid., pp.150–151)*

This frank admission that the natural law argument against homosexual acts also rules out chewing gum for pleasure nicely illustrates the folly of putting moral weight on the ill-formed notion of actions that instrumentalise the body.

None of the arguments for the moral standard 'do not engage in homosexual acts' stands up to rational scrutiny. Subscription to the standard is therefore unjustified: it is not a matter on which there is room for reasonable disagreement among reasonable people. When moral educators tackle the topic, their teaching should be directive: they should aim to bring it about that children see what is wrong with moral objections to homosexuality and so refrain from endorsing them.

In working through the three test cases in this chapter I hope to have shown that the challenge of assigning standards to justificatory categories for the purposes of moral education is not insurmountable. A large number of the moral standards that occasion dispute in society will turn out, like the prohibitions on giving offence and going private, to be of uncertain justificatory status. But sometimes disputes about moral standards are rationally unfounded: they persist despite the fact that the standards in question are demonstrably justified or unjustified. Ensuring that standards are assigned to the right justificatory categories is a matter of looking to see whether the arguments on one side or the other are decisive. This requires care and time, but the task is not so onerous as to be a serious impediment to the enterprise of rational moral education.

8

THE UNLOVELINESS OF MORAL EDUCATION

I have argued in this book that a central aim of moral education – that of bringing it about that children subscribe to moral standards and believe them to be justified – is defensible and realisable. There is a set of conflict-averting and cooperation-sustaining standards to which full moral commitment can and should be cultivated. By means of moral formation, educators should bring it about that children intend and incline to comply with these standards, want and expect everyone else to comply with them, and endorse penalties for non-compliance; and by means of directive moral inquiry, they should bring it about that children understand the reasons for intending, expecting and endorsing these things.

Some readers, I suspect, will feel a sense of unease about this core moral educational task, even if they are persuaded by the arguments I have advanced for it. The cause of their unease will not be an inability to see why compliance with moral standards is so important, but a reticence about inducing in children some of the uglier emotions and dispositions involved in moral subscription. In particular, punishing children for wrongdoing with a view to their learning to self-punish, and modelling reactions to the wrongdoing of others with a view to their learning to condemn, are pedagogical interventions with understandably little appeal to most educators. In this final chapter I should like to address the worry that moral education, in the form I have defended it, is a rather unpleasant business.

One philosopher who has pressed this worry about accounts of moral education that focus on compliance with rules is John White. He puts the point like this:

> Children are brought up to believe that ineluctable duties are laid on them to do or refrain from this or that, the content varying according to the moral system in question. They also learn, as part of this same scheme of thought, to feel guilt and remorse when they fail to live up to their obligations. They come to blame themselves for their shortcomings. And not only themselves.

They are trained to see other people, too, through the same reductive spectacles, as abiders by, or deviants from, their moral duties. The combination of rigid adherence to favoured values, unwillingness to compromise, and the pervasive tendency to blame oneself and others for moral defects is a familiar feature of our contemporary ethical landscape, not least perhaps in Britain. But our ethical life does not *have* to be as unlovely as this.

(White, 1990, p.53)

For White, then, rule-based moral education puts too much emphasis on 'the place of guilt and blame in ethical learning' (ibid., p.52). The penalty-endorsing character of subscription to moral standards necessitates an educational focus on punishment and the constellation of attitudes that accompany it. Children must acquire a vivid sense of the requirements of morality, must fear the consequences of falling short of them, must feel guilty when they do fall short, and must be ready to condemn the shortfallings of others. But if, in morally educating children, we are hemming them in with moral rules and filling their lives with fear, guilt and condemnation, should we not at least consider the possibility that we are doing them a disservice?

In what follows I shall offer two kinds of response to this worry. The first is to admit that the accusation of unloveliness has some force: the ugliness of some moral emotions is a bullet that has to be bitten by the defender of rational moral education. The second response, though, is to put up some resistance to the charge: notwithstanding the prominence it gives to guilt and blame, rational moral education is not nearly as unlovely as White suggests.

Owning the unloveliness

Let us begin by reminding ourselves of the problem-of-sociality justification for subscription to basic moral standards. There are some contingent but permanent features of the human condition – rough equality, limited sympathy and moderate scarcity of resources – whose combination is a recipe for trouble. Because we are roughly equal, we are each capable of harming others and vulnerable to harm at their hands; because our sympathies are limited, we care more about the safety and happiness of ourselves and our loved ones than about the safety and happiness of others; and because resources are moderately scarce, we are forced into competition with each other for access to goods in short supply. These features of our condition give human social groups a standing propensity to outbreaks of conflict and breakdowns in cooperation.

To recognise that human social groups have this propensity is not to deny that we all have perfectly good non-moral reasons for cooperating with each other and avoiding conflict with each other. We want our lives to go well and, other things being equal, we want other people's lives to go well too. We readily see how everyone is advantaged by cooperative schemes and disadvantaged by aggression and war. Much of the time, our self-interested and altruistic reasons are in alignment, and suffice to motivate peaceful and productive social interaction. But they are not *always* in alignment and they do not *always* suffice: rough equality, limited sympathy and moderate scarcity of resources combine to drive wedges of hostility and suspicion between us, to make us go on the offensive, withdraw trust and renege on agreements, even in the knowledge that we are thereby contributing to the very threats we fear.

And the threats are serious ones. Once trust is withdrawn, cooperative schemes soon founder; and once aggression is initiated, conflict soon escalates. If cooperation cannot be sustained, warns Hobbes, we stand to lose industry and culture, navigation and building, arts and letters. And if conflict cannot be averted, we face 'continuall feare, and danger of violent death', and lives that are 'solitary, poore, nasty, brutish, and short' (Hobbes, 1929 [1651], p.97).

Morality solves, or at least ameliorates, the problem of sociality by giving us a powerful, supplementary kind of motivation for keeping to agreements and refraining from attack. If I subscribe (morally or otherwise) to conflict-averting and cooperation-sustaining standards, I am conatively, affectively and behaviourally disposed to comply with them. And if I *morally* subscribe to those standards, I am disposed to see non-compliance with them as liable to punishment. That is to say, I am inclined to punish myself and expect condemnation from others when I fail to comply with the standards, and I am ready to punish or condemn others when they fail to comply. Morality serves to protect human social groups by motivating us to resist the self-interested reasons, uncharitable suspicions and aggressive impulses that permanently endanger them; and it achieves this by attaching some additional, and heavy, social and psychological costs to acting on those reasons, suspicions and impulses.

The point of this reminder is that salient moral emotions *have* to be ugly if they are to do the work required of them. The prospect of feeling guilty or ashamed for breaching a moral standard, or of being blamed or condemned for it by others, must be unpleasant enough to dissuade us from it, even when strongly tempted or sorely provoked. And guilt, shame, blame and condemnation are only unpleasant in prospect because they are unpleasant in fact. It is because we *do* sometimes fail to meet our moral obligations, and because we are censured and made to feel ashamed of ourselves when it happens, that we know how much we want to avoid these things. If what psychologists call the 'self-conscious' and 'other-condemning' moral emotions (Haidt, 2003) are to be effective deterrents, we must at some point experience their ugliness in full force.

And, of course, the unloveliness of moral emotions hardly compares with the unloveliness of the conduct it is their function to prevent. Violence, theft, deception, cruelty and injustice blight human lives much more profoundly than guilt and blame. If, by judiciously cultivating the latter, we can significantly reduce incidence of the former, the price is a small one to pay.

So my first reply to the accusation of unloveliness is simply to concede it: it is thoroughly unpleasant to be blamed or condemned, and to be made to feel guilty or ashamed, and for that reason most of us go out of our way to avoid it. That is precisely the mechanism by which morality solves the problem of sociality.

Not exaggerating the unloveliness

Still, I think White exaggerates the unloveliness of moral education. We should not accept too readily the picture he paints of young lives marred by a surfeit of guilt and blame. Here he is again:

> We have gone well over the top in Britain in our traditional attachment to morality and our perennial demands for moral renewal … Children are brought up on a diet of oughts. Virtually all primary school pupils know, or think they know, that they shouldn't be cheeky, should do what teacher says, shouldn't tell fibs, should keep their promises. They are brought up in a world full of stringent demands like these, with associated feelings of uneasy conscience when they transgress them … How can we want to inflict more morality on them? They have it up to here.
>
> *(White, 1997a, p.14)*

White's complaint about the 'diet of oughts' on which children are raised is not just that some moral emotions are ugly. It is that 'stringent demands' and 'feelings of uneasy conscience' set the tone of children's lives. The world they inhabit is so filled with moral obligations and emotions that we should feel sorry for them, and recoil at the idea of adding to their moral burden. But is this really how things are – or how they would be if the scheme of moral education outlined in Chapter Six were to be implemented in homes and schools?

It is certainly true that morality *can* dominate human lives to a troubling degree. This can happen in at least two ways. First, a moral code can be unduly *demanding*, with the consequence that those who share it are forever falling short of its requirements and so get little respite from the self-conscious and other-condemning emotions. Second, a moral code can be unduly *extensive*, with the consequence that those who share it must devote nearly all their time and energy to meeting its requirements, leaving little room in their lives for other things. Demandingness and extensiveness are, of course, easy bedfellows: a code that specifies what is to be done in all or most situations is quite likely to be one whose demands are difficult to meet. But it should be clear enough that these are two different ways in which morality can threaten to engulf us. The question, then, is whether the set of conflict-averting and cooperation-sustaining standards to which moral subscription is robustly justified qualifies as either very demanding or very extensive.

I contend that it does not. With respect to demandingness, most of us most of the time do not find it difficult to comply with the prohibitions and requirements of basic morality. We learn at an early age to avoid causing harm and to deal with one another honestly and fairly, and thereafter live quite comfortably within these parameters. We do not wrestle daily with our consciences about whether to save up for a new bike or just steal one, about whether to study for a test or just cheat on it. Because we subscribe to moral standards that prohibit them, stealing and cheating are not live options for us: we exclude them from the range of possibilities we are considering. And because, in the main, other members of society also habitually comply with basic moral standards, we are not much exercised by the problem of 'diffidence', by the fear that others will harm, deceive or betray us and the temptation to defend ourselves by striking first.

This is not to say that moral compliance is *never* difficult: sometimes it is very hard indeed to meet our moral obligations, and to set aside the worry that others may not meet theirs. Sometimes we fall short, and sometimes we must endure the shortfallings of others. And on these occasions we cannot escape the guilt, shame, blame and condemnation attendant on moral wrongdoing. But, where basic moral standards have currency in society, meeting their requirements is not *usually* difficult, and failures to comply are not so common as to keep us perpetually in thrall to ugly moral emotions. Life would be unpleasant indeed if its keynote emotions were shame and disapproval; but lives regulated by the conflict-averting and cooperation-sustaining standards of basic morality are simply not like that.

And nor is basic morality very extensive. It places important constraints on our freedom: there are some specific kinds of action from which we must always refrain, and some circumstances in which specific kinds of action are required of us. But within these constraints our scope to make decisions and plans in light of our goals, preferences and non-moral standards is vast. Relatively few of the decisions we make are moral ones, and even where morality bears on our decisions, it normally serves only to rule out certain options: the remaining, morally permissible options are ours to choose from. And, again, the time and effort required to fulfil our moral duties is ordinarily minimal. If all has gone well with our moral formation, we do what morality requires of us readily and habitually: we rarely spend time weighing up the pros and cons of refraining from assault, theft, deception and discrimination, even if we are momentarily tempted by these things. Compliance with basic moral standards neither takes up so much of our time, nor interferes with so many of our decisions, as to warrant the accusation that it dominates our lives.

White pays particular attention to one basic moral standard: the requirement to help those in need. Attempting to comply with this standard, he worries, can easily expand to fill every waking hour. He writes:

> the positive injunction to help others in distress is also generally recognised. Everyone will accept that this includes cases of immediacy, of sudden disaster in the here-and-now, such as when someone falls into a canal or is knocked over by a car. More distant sudden disasters are more controversial. What should one's reaction be to catastrophic flooding in another part of one's country? Or to famine on another continent? ... And what of chronic, rather than immediate distress, either local or more distant? What should one's moral stance be towards poverty, ignorance, ill-health, insecurity – and in what degrees?

> *(White, 1990, p.38)*

If the standard is interpreted in a 'maximalist' way, as requiring subscribers to take responsibility for the alleviation of all human need, immediate and chronic, local and distant, it leaves little room for anything else: it 'moralizes the whole of one's life' (ibid., p.43). Here it does begin to look as though the requirements of basic morality are unduly extensive, and unduly demanding too. The task of alleviating all human need is not only one that can take up a great deal of time and energy, but one to which none of us is adequate: if we must punish ourselves and others for every failure to relieve suffering, we are in for a bumpy emotional ride.

The answer to this worry is that the interpretation of the moral requirement to help those in need vindicated by the problem-of-sociality justification is not the maximalist interpretation. The vindicated interpretation is better captured by Bentham's formulation of the duty to rescue: 'Every man is bound to assist those who have need of assistance, if he can do it without exposing himself to sensible inconvenience' (Bentham, 2005 [1843], p.164). In other words, what basic morality requires is that we help those in need when helping is readily within our power and does not expose us to significant risk or cost. Under normal circumstances, when we are not ourselves incapacitated or in haste, we should help people up when they fall, support them when they are struggling to cope, alert them to imminent threats and assist them with heavy burdens. The standard applies principally to what White calls 'cases of immediacy': we must help our neighbours when we notice that they are in trouble and when we are in a position to do something about it.

Ameliorating the problem of sociality requires that we stand ready to assist one another in times of need because this readiness underpins our cooperative endeavours. Recall Mackie's diffident farmers, each unwilling to help the other harvest his corn for fear that the help may not be reciprocated, with the result that both lose their crops 'for want of mutual confidence and security' (Mackie, 1977, p.111). The relations of trust necessary to sustain cooperation in human social groups depend not only on people being fair, honest and reliable in their dealings with one another, but also on their willingness to extend each other a helping hand when one is needed. By contrast, it is *not* a requirement of mutual confidence and security that people commit themselves to the global project of alleviating all human need.

None of this is to deny that high ethical ideals of altruism and charity have much to commend them. Such ideals may even be necessary to flourishing human lives. The point here is that they do not belong to the set of conflict-averting and cooperation-sustaining standards to which universally-enlisting and penalty-endorsing subscription is justified. They are not standards to which we have good reason to hold ourselves and each other on pain of punishment. If moral education involved the attempt to make children feel guilty about their own, and condemnatory about others', failures to comply with a standard of unrestricted altruism, it would indeed be an unlovely thing.

So White's worry about moral education filling children's lives with guilt and blame is unfounded, at least insofar as the content of moral formation and directive moral inquiry is confined to the set of standards needed to ameliorate the problem of sociality. Basic morality is neither very demanding nor very extensive: most of us meet its requirements without much difficulty and with plenty of time to spare.

Unfortunately, White anticipates this rebuttal of his primary charge against moral education and lines up a secondary one. There is, he suggests, *also* something unlovely about cultivating subscription to a moral code that is *not* demanding or extensive. The problem he sees with moral standards that are easily satisfied is that they give tacit support to hedonistic or self-interested ways of life. Responding to an earlier and briefer formulation of the theory set out in this book, White levels just this charge against it:

> If Hand is indeed advocating a minimalist morality as the hub of his theory of moral education, this lands him in a difficulty. He has constructed his theory in order to base moral education on a non-controversial foundation. While it is, granted, non-controversial that children should be taught to tell the truth, and not to steal, or break promises, this is true only of these injunctions when taken individually. If one puts them together in such a way as to form a minimalist morality, controversy enters the scene. For not everyone, by any means, would agree that children should be brought up in so morally undemanding a way – a way that permits, for those so inclined, so self-centred an existence.
>
> *(White, 2016, p.451)*

This new objection is a little dispiriting. White's original worry was that children are at risk of being morally overburdened, so one might have expected him to be reassured by the news that the moral standards to be cultivated are not onerous. Instead he is immediately beset by another, contrary worry, to the effect that easy-to-meet moral requirements allow children to be selfish with impunity. The prospects of setting his mind at rest begin to look bleak.

Still, it is worth asking what lies behind White's association of basic morality with self-centredness. It is tautologously true that, once people have done everything morality requires of them, they are morally permitted to devote the rest of their waking hours to narrowly self-interested pursuits. But from the fact that they are morally permitted to do this, it hardly follows that this is all they have reason to do, or all they will want to do. It is not as if the only two motivators of human action are moral duty and narrow self-interest. So what leads White to fear that those who subscribe to a 'minimalist morality' will be tempted by a 'self-centred existence'? His thought appears to be that, although moral duty and narrow self-interest are not the only springs of action, they are the springs that loom largest in societies shaped by the Christian tradition. He elaborates the point in another essay on moral education:

> A difficulty has been that the religious tradition has bequeathed us no real picture of what a personally fulfilled life could be like except in terms of

devotion to God and one's moral duties. Apart from this there are only the pleasures and temptations of our animal nature – held to be a common but false picture of a happy life, from which Duty alone can rescue us.

(White, 1997b, p.24)

On White's view, then, Christianity has given us only two pictures of happiness: the kind that lies in devotion to moral duty and the kind that lies in the pursuit of animal pleasure. And whereas the Christian idea was that we should choose between these paths, many of us today see our lives as a balancing act between the two:

> What I suspect has happened in a lot of cases is that people still have something like the traditional moral beliefs that they shouldn't harm others in the usual ways – lying, stealing etc. – but that since most of these are about things to *refrain* from, it's perfectly possible to live out one's life within these moral rules, yet spend an enormous proportion of it on one's own pursuits. Paradoxically, it is through their attachment to something not so far removed from traditional morality that some people in our society – how many I don't know – seem to enjoy, strive for or dream of some version of the old religious view of the *dolce vita* of physical comforts and pleasures – sex, suntan and Sangria, electronic paradises, nice houses and nice gardens, coming up on the Lottery, villas in Spain or the south of France.
>
> *(ibid., p.25)*

There is, to be sure, something unlovely about the vision of human flourishing White sketches here. Lives dedicated exclusively to meeting the requirements of basic morality and enjoying the pleasures of sex, suntan and Sangria are impoverished ones indeed. If moral education of the kind I am defending were somehow implicated in advocacy of this vision, White would have legitimate grounds for complaint.

But it is emphatically not so implicated. There is no connection at all between cultivating moral subscription to conflict-averting and cooperation-sustaining standards and promoting the pursuit of pleasure and self-interest. Indeed, the justification for basic morality set out in Chapter Five depends on the assumption that human beings are *not* narrowly self-interested: it is not at all clear that contractarianism can survive the Gauthierian theoretical constraint of 'mutual unconcern' (Gauthier, 1986). It is precisely because we are sympathetic to one another, because we are moved by others' suffering, because we want everyone to be happy and healthy and safe, that we have good reason to subscribe (and not just feign subscription) to moral standards. Far from being implied or encouraged by pedagogical endorsement of the problem-of-sociality justification for morality, thoroughgoing self-centredness sits most uneasily with it.

White's diagnosis of our cultural plight is fairly unpersuasive. The choice with which the Christian tradition presents us is not accurately represented as a choice between moral duty and animal pleasures. It is a choice between the spirit and the flesh, where 'the fruit of the spirit is love, joy, peace, patience, kindness, goodness, faithfulness, gentleness, self-control' (Galatians 5: 22–23). The kind of happiness Christianity commends to us lies not just in devotion to moral duty, but in loving relationships with one another and with God. The life of the spirit is as much about compassion and companionship as it is about compliance. And, in any case, Christianity is not the only formative influence on our cultural inheritance. Our thinking about the good life is shaped at least as significantly by the ancient Greeks and the ideas that flourishing might consist in rational activity, or the contemplation of eternal truths, or the exercise of human excellences. The suggestion that we are culturally so in thrall to a grim caricature of Christianity that we struggle to recognise any reasons to act besides moral obligation and physical desire is more than a little odd.

Moreover, even if White's cultural diagnosis were accurate, it would hardly follow that 'minimalist' moral education is part of the problem, or that the situation could be improved by making morality more demanding. Merely adjusting the balance between duty and self-interest does nothing to restore the neglected springs of action to their rightful place. If, as a society, we have lost sight of the worthwhile goals we might pursue once our moral duties have been discharged, the solution is to rediscover those goals and to ensure that children are made vividly aware of them. We must seek out and make available to children the rich panoply of non-hedonic goods that can contribute to well-lived lives. That may involve some significant reshaping of the school curriculum, but it has no bearing on the content of moral education.

Notwithstanding his separate objections to excessively and insufficiently demanding forms of moral education, White is not hankering after a golden mean between the two. His recommendation is that we replace rule-based moral education with something else entirely. We should, he thinks, 'focus directly on altruistic, rather than moral, educational aims' and concentrate our efforts on 'the cultivation of altruistic dispositions' (White, 1990, pp.45–46). He construes altruism as 'a lively concern for the well-being of other people with whom we live, work and form communities' (ibid., p.41) and proposes that we nurture the dispositions of 'being attached to those close to one', 'having warm relationships with those with whom one comes into frequent contact', 'being well-disposed to strangers with whom one has face-to-face contact', and 'being disposed to protect others' well-being in general' (ibid., p.47). This sort of sympathy-cultivating education is, he thinks, a significant improvement on teaching children to subscribe to moral standards.

But it is a serious mistake to see these two endeavours as alternatives between which we must choose. Educators can and should do what they can to enhance children's sympathy for others and to help them appreciate the great value in human lives of intimate relationships, warm friendships and supportive communities. They should also bring it about that children subscribe to the moral standards needed to avert conflict and sustain cooperation in human social groups. These undertakings are complementary and mutually reinforcing: sympathy for others serves to justify and reinforce commitment to moral standards, and commitment to moral standards provides the stable social conditions in which friendships and communities can flourish.

And it would be an even more serious mistake to suppose that cultivating altruistic dispositions might be sufficient on its own to solve the problem of sociality. Children's sympathies can certainly be educationally extended, but they cannot be so far extended as to change the circumstances of justice. That our sympathies are limited is a permanent feature of the human condition: no educational intervention can overcome our tendency to prioritise the safety and happiness of ourselves and our loved ones over the safety and happiness of others. It is this fact of our nature, along with our rough equality and a moderate scarcity of resources, that generates the need for a system of moral constraints. Enhanced altruism can make it easier for people to meet the demands of morality, and can move them to do more for each other than morality requires; but it cannot make morality redundant.

I conclude that the unloveliness charges White levels against rational moral education are largely misplaced. The basic moral standards to which subscription is to be cultivated are not so demanding or so extensive as to fill children's lives with ugly moral emotions. And the fact that basic morality is relatively undemanding does not imply that teaching it gives tacit support to hedonistic or self-interested ways of life. It may well be the case that more attention should be given in schools to acquainting children with worthwhile goals and to enlarging their sympathies, but such attention is quite compatible with, and certainly does not obviate the need for, rational moral education.

Pace Kant, the moral law within is not really a thing of beauty. Morality, one might say, is a dirty tool for a dirty job: violence, deception and injustice must be curbed, and shame and condemnation are ways of curbing them. But the job is a vital one and morality is the best tool we have. The stability of human social groups depends on subscription to moral standards, so each generation must take responsibility for cultivating the subscription of the next. What I have tried to show in this book is that this responsibility can be discharged without any lapse in educational propriety. Many moral standards are matters of reasonable disagreement among reasonable people, and these must be taught nondirectively, in a way that enables children to form their own considered views. Some, too, are demonstrably unjustified, and these should be taught in a way that actively discourages children from endorsing them. But there is also a set of basic moral standards that enjoy the support of a sound justificatory argument: to these it is quite proper for parents and teachers to cultivate full moral commitment, by means of moral formation and directive moral inquiry. Moral educators who take seriously the responsibility of raising morally decent children can therefore be as rational, rigorous and resolute in their aversion to indoctrination as educators of any other stripe.

REFERENCES

Aquinas, St Thomas, *Summa Contra Gentiles*, New York: Hanover House, 1955–1957, http://dhspriory.org/thomas/ContraGentiles.htm (retrieved 20/06/17).

Beauchamp, T.L. and Childress, J.F. (1994) *Principles of Biomedical Ethics* (Fourth Edition), Oxford: Oxford University Press.

Bentham, J. (2005 [1843]) *The Works of Jeremy Bentham, Volume One*, Boston: Adamant Media Corporation.

Brighouse, H. (2000) *School Choice and Social Justice*, Oxford: Oxford University Press.

Brighouse, H. and Swift, A. (2014) *Family Values: The Ethics of Parent-Child Relationships*, Princeton: Princeton University Press.

Copp, D. (2016) 'Moral education versus indoctrination', *Theory and Research in Education* 14(2), 149–167.

Copp, D. (2009) 'Toward a pluralist and teleological theory of normativity', *Philosophical Issues 19: Metaethics*, 21–37.

Copp, D. (1995) *Morality, Normativity and Society*, Oxford: Oxford University Press.

Dearden, R. (1984) *Theory and Practice in Education*, London: Routledge & Kegan Paul.

Dearden, R. (1981) 'Controversial issues and the curriculum', *Journal of Curriculum Studies* 13(1), 37–44.

D'Olimpio, L. (2017) *Media and Moral Education: A Philosophy of Critical Engagement*, London: Routledge.

Dostoevesky, F. (2010 [1880]) *The Brothers Karamazov*, Ware: Wordsworth Editions.

Feinberg, J. (1988) *Offense to Others: The Moral Limits of the Criminal Law, Volume Two*, Oxford: Oxford University Press.

Feinberg, J. (1987) *Harm to Others: The Moral Limits of the Criminal Law, Volume One*, Oxford: Oxford University Press.

Finnis, J. (1994) 'Law, morality and "sexual orientation"', *Notre Dame Law Review* 69(5), 1049–1076.

Finnis, J. and Nussbaum, M. (1993) 'Is homosexual conduct wrong? A philosophical exchange', *The New Republic*, 15 November 1993, 12–13.

Gauthier, D. (1986) *Morals by Agreement*, Oxford: Clarendon Press.

George, R.P. (1999) *In Defense of Natural Law*, Oxford: Oxford University Press.

Gowers, E. (2015) *Plain Words: A Guide to the Use of English*, London: Penguin.

Grisez, G. (1993) *The Way of the Lord Jesus, Volume Two: Living a Christian Life*, Quincy: Franciscan Press.

Haidt, J. (2003) 'The moral emotions', in Davidson, R.J., Scherer, K.R. and Goldsmith, H.H. (eds) *Handbook of Affective Sciences*, Oxford: Oxford University Press, pp.852–870.

Hand, M. (2014) 'Towards a theory of moral education', *Journal of Philosophy of Education* 48(4), 519–532.

Hand, M. (2004a) 'Religious upbringing: a rejoinder to Mackenzie, Gardner and Tan', *Journal of Philosophy of Education* 38(4), 639–648.

Hand, M. (2004b) 'The problem with faith schools: a reply to my critics', *Theory and Research in Education* 2(3), 343–353.

Hand, M. (2003) 'A philosophical objection to faith schools', *Theory and Research in Education* 1(1), 89–99.

Hand, M. (2002) 'Religious upbringing reconsidered', *Journal of Philosophy of Education* 36(4), 545–557.

Hart, H.L.A. (1994 [1961]) *The Concept of Law*, Second Edition, Oxford: Clarendon Press.

Haydon, G. (2007) 'A neglected resource for values education', *Learning for Life* 8, 10.

Haydon, G. (1999) 'Values, virtues and violence: education and the public understanding of morality', *Journal of Philosophy of Education* 33(1), 1–156.

Hobbes, T. (1929 [1651]) *Leviathan*, Oxford: Clarendon Press.

Hume, D. (1990 [1779]) *Dialogues Concerning Natural Religion*, London: Penguin.

Hume, D. (1896 [1739]) *A Treatise of Human Nature*, Oxford: Clarendon Press.

Macedo, S. (1995) 'Homosexuality and the conservative mind', *Georgetown Law Journal* 84, 261–300.

Mackie, J.L. (1977) *Ethics: Inventing Right and Wrong*, Harmondsworth: Penguin.

Mill, J.S. (1989 [1859]) *On Liberty*, Cambridge: Cambridge University Press.

Mill, J.S. (1962 [1861]) *Utilitarianism*, London: Collins.

Orwell, G. (1946) 'A nice cup of tea', *Evening Standard*, 12 January 1946, http://orwell.ru/library/articles/tea/english/e_tea (retrieved 20/06/17).

Pascal, B. (2011 [1660]) *Pensees*, Oxford: Benediction Classics.

Perry, M.J. (1995) 'The morality of homosexual conduct: a response to John Finnis', *Notre Dame Journal of Law, Ethics and Public Policy* 9(1), 41–74.

Rawls, J. (2005) *Political Liberalism* (Expanded Edition), New York: Columbia University Press.

Rawls, J. (1971) *A Theory of Justice*, Cambridge: Belknap Press.

Schools Curriculum and Assessment Authority (SCAA) (1997) 'The preamble to the statement of values' and 'The statement of values', in Smith, R. and Standish, P. (eds) *Teaching Right and Wrong: Moral Education in the Balance*, Stoke on Trent: Trentham, pp.10–14.

Schools Curriculum and Assessment Authority (SCAA) (1996) *Education for Adult Life: The Spiritual and Moral Development of Young People* (SCAA Discussion Paper No.6), London: SCAA.

Singer, P. (1975) *Animal Liberation: A New Ethics for Our Treatment of Animals*, New York: New York Review.

Swift, A. (2004) 'The morality of school choice', *Theory and Research in Education* 2(1), 7–21.

Talbot, M. and Tate, N. (1997) 'Shared values in a pluralist society?', in Smith, R. and Standish, P. (eds) *Teaching Right and Wrong: Moral Education in the Balance*, Stoke on Trent: Trentham, pp.1–9.

Warnock, G.J. (1971) *The Object of Morality*, London: Methuen.

Weckert, J. (2007) 'Giving and taking offence in a global context', *International Journal of Technology and Human Interaction* 3(3), 25–35.

White, J. (2016) 'Moral education and education in altruism: two replies to Michael Hand', *Journal of Philosophy of Education* 50(3), 448–460.

White, J. (1997a) 'Is moral education an aid or an obstacle to personal well-being?', *Prospero* 3(1), 14–17.

White, J. (1997b) 'Three proposals and a rejection', in Smith, R. and Standish, P. (eds) *Teaching Right and Wrong: Moral Education in the Balance*, Stoke on Trent: Trentham, pp.15–27.

White, J. (1990) *Education and the Good Life: Beyond the National Curriculum*, London: Kogan Page.

White, J. (1967) 'Indoctrination', in Peters, R.S. (ed.) *The Concept of Education*, London: Routledge & Kegan Paul, pp.177–191.

Williams, B. (1985) *Ethics and the Limits of Philosophy*, London: Fontana.

Wilson, J., Williams, N. and Sugarman, B. (1967) *Introduction to Moral Education*, Harmondsworth: Penguin.

Wittgenstein, L. (1953) *Philosophical Investigations*, trans. Anscombe, G.E.M., Oxford: Blackwell.

INDEX